FAT FREE
FOREVER

By the same authors
Cured to Death: The Effects of Prescription Drugs
Hayfever: No Need to Suffer
The Long-life Heart: How to Avoid Heart Disease and Live
    a Longer Life
Alternatives to Drugs
Immunity Plus

FAT FREE

FOREVER

The Natural Way to Conquer Persistent Fat

DR. ARABELLA MELVILLE
AND COLIN JOHNSON

Crown Publishers, Inc.
New York

For Inge, Colin's daughter
and
For Joan, Arabella's mother

Copyright © 1986 by Arabella Melville and Colin Johnson

All rights reserved. No part of this book may be reproduced or transmitted in any form or by any means, electronic or mechanical, including photocopying, recording, or by any information storage and retrieval system, without permission in writing from the publisher.

Published in the United States of America in 1987 by Crown Publishers, Inc., 225 Park Avenue South, New York, New York 10003 and represented in Canada by the Canadian MANDA Group.

Originally published in Great Britain under the title *Persistent Fat and How to Lose It* by Century Hutchinson Ltd., Broadmount House, 62–65 Chandos Place, Covent Garden, London WC2N 4NW.

CROWN is a trademark of Crown Publishers, Inc.

Manufactured in the United States of America

Library of Congress Cataloging-in-Publication Data

Melville, Arabella, 1948–
    Fat free forever.

    Bibliography: p.
    Includes index.
    1. Reducing diets. I. Johnson, Colin, 1938–
II. Title.
RM222.2.M452   1987   613.2′5   87-6828
ISBN 0-517-56445-9

10   9   8   7   6   5   4   3   2   1

First American Edition

Contents

1	Is This Your Problem?	1
2	What This Book Will Do for You	4
3	The Overused Calorie	8
4	Take a New Look at Fat	13
5	The PFR Syndrome	28
6	Case Histories	36
7	PFR—The Cause	43
8	Are You What You Eat?	52
9	Escape PFR—The Plan	69
10	The Diet—Innocent Food	83
11	Your Environment	108
12	Your Metabolism	122
13	Week-by-Week Action Plans	137
14	Permanent Good Shape	148
15	PFR—The Theoretical Model	155
16	The Rest of the Iceberg	167

Appendix 1   Food Additives   180
Appendix 2   Prescription Drugs That May
  Cause Weight Gain   188
Appendix 3   Organic Food Suppliers   193
Appendix 4   Basic Movement   198
Appendix 5   Organizations Working
  Toward an Unpolluted World   203
Appendix 6   Further Help   205
References   207
Acknowledgments   211
Index   213

1

Is This Your Problem?

Everyone would like to be thin and healthy. Yet in spite of advances in nutrition and the growing popularity of exercise, that happy state remains elusive for the majority of people.

We believe that the *Persistent Fat Retention (PFR) Syndrome* is at the root of this disappointment. If you have been struggling unsuccessfully for years with excess weight, flabbiness, or unsightly cellulite, you could be a victim of the PFR Syndrome.

Read on. This book is good news for you!

How can you be sure this is your problem? The difficulty with a syndrome is that it is a collection of symptoms that can be caused by a wide variety of factors. These factors will vary from one individual to another, and as you will read later, it took the power of modern computer technology to reveal the underlying pattern of causes that were producing this very common condition.

In spite of the complex causes, we can give some pointers that will help you assess its relevance to you. The crucial characteristic of persistent fat is that it resists conventional attempts to shift it by diet and exercise. It is no exaggeration to say that in many cases it resists starvation—persistent fat seems to be locked on to your body. It can be in quite small

1

areas—many otherwise thin and elegant women have it on the backs of their thighs—or it can take the form of an overall excess of fat. The position on the body and the form of fat retained varies from person to person, but its persistence is the common factor.

In very simple terms, the PFR Syndrome is caused by a substance, usually a fat-soluble chemical, that your metabolism treats as toxic. Your metabolism deals with toxins all the time, but sooner or later it will reach overload or encounter a substance it would rather not face. The system then chooses to cope with these difficult molecules by dumping them in fat. Once this strategy has been used, these substances tend to remain locked in fat, and we need to adopt specific routines, designed to release them safely, so that our metabolism can cope again in the normal way. When we have achieved this, our body will no longer require the fat, and it can be lost without difficulty.

A substance that causes fat deposition in one person may have no effect on another. You will need to use knowledge of yourself, and clues, like the timing of any sudden weight gain, to work out the degree to which the PFR Syndrome affects you.

The questionnaire below will give some pointers. The first four questions refer to common characteristics of the PFR Syndrome, while the following questions illustrate common causes. One of these factors may have precipitated your problem. If you answer a definite "yes" to two or more questions, there is a good chance that you are a victim of the PFR Syndrome.

1. Have you been dieting for much of the past few years, but still find you are carrying more fat than you should?

2. Do you develop headaches or nausea during or after exercise?

3. Is any significant weight loss followed immediately by gain—even if you don't eat excessively?

4. Do you have specific areas of fat (for example, on thighs, upper arms, belly, or hips) that persist when your body is otherwise thin?

5. Do periods of weight gain tend to coincide with allergy problems?

6. Did you put on weight during, or shortly after, taking medication for a period of time?

7. Are you taking oral contraceptives, or have you taken them in the past and given up because of side effects?

8. Are you unusually sensitive to the effects of alcohol, drugs, anesthetics, or solvents? (Signs include getting easily intoxicated, headaches, nausea, dizziness, skin rashes, asthma, and palpitations.)

9. Did you put on fat, which now persists, at the time of a major change in your life, such as a new home or job?

10. Did a weight or fat increase persist after pregnancy?

If you believe you are a PFR victim, do not despair. The revolutionary new theory in this book has the answer. The first thing you have to do is to read carefully and understand exactly what it is you are dealing with, and how you are going to get rid of that unwanted fat.

2

What This Book Will Do for You

This book is not for everyone. It is written for people who seriously wish to lose persistent fat. It accomplishes this by explaining the PFR Syndrome and putting you in charge of your body so that you can control the amount of fat you carry. Although dietary change is involved, this is not a diet book. If you are one of those unfortunate people who, for whatever psychological reason, need to diet continually without achieving anything positive, this book is not for you.

Before going any further you should ask yourself the following questions:

Do I really want to have a thin and attractive body?

Can I cope with being in control of my body?

Am I absolutely sure I am not hiding behind fat and failure?

If you can say an emphatic "yes!" to any two of these questions, then you will gain a lot from reading this book. Here is what it will do for you.

It will show you how to lose persistent fat. By this we mean not only ordinary body fat but also cellulite and that unhealthy, watery flab, those unwanted tissues that resist all the reducing methods you may have previously tried.

Beyond this, it may also explain problems of clinical obesity, both in adults and children.

It will teach you how to maintain your body at your desired weight for the rest of your life with methods that are progressive, natural, and entirely safe.

It will enhance your looks because it will improve that essential foundation of all beauty, inner health.

It will introduce you to the holistic concepts of living that lie behind the method of dealing with the Persistent Fat Retention Syndrome.

And once you have lost your persistent weight, it will teach you how to achieve the sort of body shape you desire.

Finally it will explain why many of the other methods of weight loss you may have tried have failed to achieve permanent results, and why many of them may actually damage your health and contribute to your unwanted fat problem.

We accept that if you have been seeking these ideals before, you will be used to such apparently excessive claims. Over the years they have all been heard from less than scrupulous practitioners.

We have been successfully helping a wide range of people to deal with this problem for some time. It is this experience that makes us sure that we are not making extravagant claims. But you must not be under the illusion that we can do it for you. This book will explain what is happening to you and why; it will teach you how to control the factors that lead to PFR, and how to lose that unwanted weight—but you have to do it yourself!

Let us start by telling how we discovered the PFR Syndrome.

We run a computer-based health and personal-growth system, Life Profile Ltd. Basically, what it does is to ask clients what sort of state they are in, and what sort of condition they would like to achieve. We were able to produce this book because the Life Profile computers uncovered a series of very similar patterns for clients with weight-loss problems that had common features. Computers are very good at pinpointing such patterns.

In providing individual programs for slimming down and losing weight, we noticed two things. One we had anticipated; but the other was a surprise. The first was the problem that everyone who tries to lose weight by dieting alone quickly discovers: while you can lose weight in this way, keeping it off is very difficult. We decided to avoid diets in the conventional sense, concentrating instead on guiding people toward a healthy, balanced way of eating. To enable them to lose weight, we adjusted their life patterns and activity levels. By and large, this is a successful strategy; most of our clients achieved their desired weights and physical conditions and found little difficulty in maintaining them.

But at the same time, there were clients who, whatever we recommended, could not lose weight, or could not keep it off. Most were women who, although no more likely than men to suffer from weight problems, are generally more aware of them and find it more difficult to lose fat. We have aimed this book primarily at women, because they are more likely to become victims of PFR for reasons that will be explained later. However, men too can suffer from PFR, and it is likely that the same mechanism is capable of producing other serious effects in men; these are explored in the last chapter.

Every now and then, clients would report sudden weight increases that occurred over a fairly short period of time and for no obvious reason. They accumulated body fat at what was for them an alarming rate.

We knew that this tended to happen to conventional dieters; the whole seesaw of weight loss followed predictably by weight gain was exposed in *Dieting Makes You Fat,* by Geoffrey Cannon and Hetty Einzig. But our system had been specifically designed both to cope with individual variability and to avoid this trap. So what was going wrong?

Two things stood out. Some people proved unable to keep fat off, even if they ate almost nothing at all. And some people who appeared to have solved their body weight problem would suddenly put on excess weight. This weight increase happened for no reason we could explain, and to further complicate matters, once this mystery fat had been gained, it was very difficult to lose.

Obviously something was happening that had not been suspected before. We started to isolate the data we had on clients who seemed to be victims, to see if we could identify the cause. We called the problem the PFR Syndrome—Persistent Fat Retention—because that is exactly what it is.

We read many books and scientific papers in our search for clues. An outline of the problem was sent to experts who have contributed to the Life Profile data base. It's a little like asking all your friends to give you ten pieces of their favorite jigsaw puzzle, and then trying to put them all together! Nevertheless a faint pattern did begin to emerge.

The clues are obvious now, as in all solved puzzles. The reports of DDT being found in the fat of arctic seals; the mysterious mass deaths of seabirds on migratory flights; a sentence in *Dieting Makes You Fat:* "For a while a series of malaises and infections made me feel as if running were in some way literally jogging poisons in my body to the surface," which had echoes in the experiences of some Life Profile clients. And the key was staring us in the face.

Arabella, an expert in pharmacology, has extensive knowledge of the adverse effects of prescription drugs. Indeed our first book, *Cured to Death: The Effects of Prescription Drugs,* is an exposé of the horrifying situation revealed by her research in this field. But it was not until one of our clients gave us information that connected her dramatic accumulation of fat with a particular drug treatment that the whole puzzle fell into place.

After careful checking and consultation, we developed a new program for those Life Profile clients who were victims of the PFR Syndrome. It solved the problem. This book is the result of this work; we believe that if you are one of the millions of people who struggle continually with unwanted fat, who find no permanent answer on the diet seesaw, who discover that whatever activity they try does not work, you could be a victim of the PFR Syndrome. This is your answer!

3

The Overused Calorie

It is a startling fact that our whole society is eating less than ever before. Over the past two decades the average calorie consumption per day in the United States has dropped 5 percent. The textbooks on food requirements have to be periodically revised as the statistics prove that we can live on much less than the experts proclaimed.

Yet, at the same time, people are getting fatter and heavier than ever before. In 1980, a woman of average height (5 feet 4 inches) weighed ten pounds more than she would have in 1930 or 1943. Men, too, have gained close to fifteen pounds on the average. This increase represents the greater quantity of fat now burdening our bodies. In the United States the average person has 10 percent more fat than twenty years ago!

Although there are many individual exceptions to this general picture, it represents an undeniable trend with each of us accumulating fat as time goes by. Americans are turning into a nation of chubbies. Yet the superficial observer would expect exactly the opposite.

Around a hundred million Americans diet. Two out of every three women are either dieting or between one diet and the next. And in spite of the fact that that dieting is not an effective answer, more and more men are joining the self-depriving and suffering hordes. On top of this, millions have taken up exercise. Amateur athletes and dancers gyrate and burn; panting joggers pound the streets; and every town worth its salt substitute has its marathon.

According to the conventional wisdom, all of this effort and activity should be reducing our weight. We are taught that the fewer calories you eat, the less fat you will put on. Obesity experts, the billion-dollar weight-loss industry, and most of the population are in agreement: the way to get thin is by following a low-calorie diet.

Not only is this simplistic nonsense, as most of us know from bitter experience, but as we show later, it is a view that has many dangers to health and no advantages. The truth is that, for many of us, the fat we carry is only very loosely connected to our calorie intake, whether this is excessive or not. The usual result is that, even though a reduction in food intake is reflected in short-term weight loss, that weight goes right back on—often in greater quantities—the second willpower fails or something disrupts the diet obsession.

For those who have added exercise to their ammunition in the fight against flab, the situation is frequently not much better. They may be more fit, but are they less fat? Many people find that, in spite of burning calories by the score, they stay fatter than they would like. They put on weight, because the physical effort to burn off fat becomes so great that they find they are building muscle. Such a weight-loss routine needs to be very finely tuned and as obsessively followed as the weight-loss diet for any hope of success.

The exerciser's hopes are dashed almost as frequently as those of the dieter. Why is this? Although exercise and activity have much to recommend them, as main parts of a conventional weight-loss strategy they are limited by the same mistaken theory that governs dieting: input in calories must be less than output in energy. We are back to the simple old calorie equation that fails for large numbers of people.

The calorie-fat equation is not merely inadequate, but for any hope of success, no matter how limited, it demands total dedication. It requires dieters who seriously accept calorie control as their means of salvation to become quite literally obsessed.

But thinness should not be such a difficult thing to achieve. Humans are naturally active animals, and we would not have achieved our position as the dominant species unless we could live a naturally healthy life without becoming excessively fat. There is no doubt that we are more fit and healthier if we are thin; this is our optimal natural state.

Our body has a whole range of complex and subtle mechanisms for maintaining all its systems at their best constant level. Our temperature is the best example; it varies only when something is going wrong. Similarly, our body weight will tend to be maintained at a level that is naturally best for us. There will be seasonal variations, a little fat to carry us through the winter, and changes that fit our changing roles as we grow older. But by and large our capacity for homeostasis will dictate that we tend to revert to our best natural weight.

So what is going wrong? The dieter's obsessive fight to override the body's efforts to put on fat seems to show that what our bodies think best is in direct conflict with our beliefs and wishes. Fighting to assert your desire in preference to your body's priority is bound to be damaging to health.

A wild exaggeration? We don't think so. The harm is caused by a basic misunderstanding of what happens to your body when you try to lose fat, whether by dieting or by combining diet and exercise. Instead of your efforts reducing fat, they cause the body to metabolize lean tissues. Why should the body behave so apparently illogically? If fat were simply a passive store of excess calories, why should valuable and active tissue from muscles and vital organs be shed before fat?

By not asking these questions, all those who have offered answers to dieters have been missing a major point. Fat must be far more than an accidental accumulation that happens to annoy us, and that we can casually get rid of.

Searching for diets that will allow dieters to believe they can eat more yet weigh less, by choosing to eat substances that pass through digestive tracts with minimal effect, is a hopeless task. These diets ignore the physiological needs that are fulfilled by correct nourishment, and assume that our metabolic processes are easily fooled. Similarly, those who offer a way of changing or correcting supposed metabolic imbalances with medicines or other substances are clutching at straws. The trend, where the metabolic processes of millions of individuals are actually fighting to maintain fat, if necessary at the expense of lean tissue, is unlikely to be affected by such tinkering.

Nor has conventional medicine been of much help to those who have ended up with severe obesity problems. Most doctors are locked in the calories-equals-fat era. In desperation some have resorted to wiring shut the jaws of overweight patients. When people agree to be treated in this way, surely something is desperately wrong with our understanding, both of ourselves and of what is happening to us.

The problem of excess weight is not limited to those who want to look good on the beach. By the age of eleven, when most children are stringy as beanpoles, 8 percent of boys and 10 percent of girls are more than 20 percent over the normal reference weight for their height. According to *Nutrition Reviews*, a U.S. journal, the average weight of Americans for their height is continuing to rise. We think it would be difficult to blame this on bad eating habits in the accepted sense.

There are signs that some professionals in the field are beginning to come to terms with the puzzles of our increasing weight. In the *International Journal of Obesity*, G. A. Bray noted that "obesity may be a collection of diseases with multiple etiology." In other words, many things can cause obesity. The cynical interpretation of this remark would be that it is an admission both that the experts have had it wrong, and that they admit they do not understand. A more positive view is that it accepts that people are all different, and will be affected by different things in different ways. Unless a solution to unwanted weight addresses this fact, it is likely to fail.

Our increasing problems with fat have many puzzling features. Even the British Royal College of Physicians has recently admitted that "the traditional view that the majority of overweight subjects are eating more or exercising less than those of a normal weight is now recognized as not being uniformly true." But until we have a clearer picture of reality, we are not likely to be able to solve the problem.

Although we must not forget the importance of individual differences, we can identify some general features that apply to the overweight population as a whole. For millions, efforts at weight loss based on conventional understanding of the body's fat mechanisms fail. We are eating less, yet weighing more. Many people find that they can put on large amounts of fat at an alarming rate. If pressured into losing weight, the body will frequently shed healthy, lean tissue rather than apparently inert fat. Excess fat is neither healthy nor natural, but our bodies insist on creating and maintaining it.

So what are we to conclude?

The answer seems inescapable. Something is causing our bodies to believe that it is in their best interests to put on fat. And whatever forces promote this are already widespread and becoming increasingly common.

The questions we now have to answer are these. Why do our bodies need this extra fat? What is the mechanism that forces them to maintain it? And what can we do about it?

The answers are in the rest of this book.

4

Take a New Look at Fat

This chapter is not intended to persuade you to come to terms with your fat or to accept your body as it is. Thin people do tend to be healthier and more successful, and we should all aim to be at our optimal weight with no unnecessary fat. But as we concluded in the last chapter, our bodies seem to believe quite emphatically that they need fat—much more fat than makes sense to us. And our metabolic systems will go to extreme lengths to produce or preserve our fat.

To understand why this is so, we need to look at the reasons our bodies have for making fat. There is no substitute for detailed knowledge of your enemy!

Fat cells are laid down very early in life, mostly before we are born. When our weight increases in adulthood, these cells are pumped up with fat and water; we don't actually grow new ones, but rather, those we have are filled. They have an enormous capacity for expansion.

Fat has a wide range of functions in our lives, ranging from effects on the physiology and psychology of reproduction to the molecular management of our metabolism. The amount of fat we carry depends on the mixture of its functions that are important to us as individuals at any particular time, balanced

13

against the costs to our bodies of maintaining extra weight. This is a complex interaction which will vary according to circumstances and at each stage of our lives.

To simplify the picture we can split fat functions into four areas. These are:

1. Sexual attraction
2. Insulation
3. Food storage
4. Neutralization of poisons

While the first three may be familiar to you, it is the fourth function that is at the heart of the problem of persistent fat retention. The discovery that fat has this function is entirely new. It is the crucial explanation for the fat and cellulite problems experienced by so many people. It explains the puzzles of the previous chapter.

But it would be misleading, not to say irresponsible, if we were to encourage you to think that armed with an understanding of this function you could solve your weight problem. All of the functions of fat will be important to you to some degree. And the importance of each to you will have a different emphasis from that for your friend, sister, or mother. Because we are each so different as individuals, no single, simple answer will work for us all. What we must aim for is our own answer, with the right *balance* of each of these functions for our needs. With the balance right, we can then safely lose fat and be thin and healthy.

FAT AND SEXUAL ATTRACTION

In our culture we tend to overlook the fact that fat plays an important part in making women sexually attractive. We understand that too much fat has the opposite effect, but if you had no fat at all, the effect would be quite horrible. The rounded and shapely contours displayed by models are formed by that subcutaneous layer of fat peculiar to the female; and breasts, the definition of femininity, are almost entirely composed of fatty tissues.

It is well known that some African and Arabian societies have taken the sexual implications of fat to the extreme. For them the fatter the bride, the more her worth; and dances and displays have been devised to show off plump behinds or well-covered bellies to best advantage. And whatever the public attitudes of our culture, it remains true that large women seem to have little difficulty in attracting men.

The dieter's disease, anorexia nervosa, is a growing phenomenon which reflects deep and widespread problems with self-acceptance, especially among adolescent girls. The changes in a young girl's body shape with maturity act as signals. To males, the girl's accumulation of fatty tissue in the "right" places says "I am sexually mature and ready to be approached." To other females, the message will be "I am no longer a child; I am ready to be treated as an equal." Such messages are not always welcomed because they indicate irrevocable change both for the individual and for her social relationships with those around her. When combined with other indicators, the growth of body hair and the beginning of menstruation, the whole experience can be quite overwhelming. This is especially difficult to deal with when it happens against a background of heavy parental inhibition and sexual guilt, or an antagonistic relationship between mother and daughter.

The girl is driven into maturity by forces outside her control. But at some level she is aware of the role of fat; it is the re-shaper of her girlish, innocent body, and periods and fertility only occur when she achieves a certain height/weight ratio. Without fully understanding these processes, she can perceive that the unwanted changes are associated with fat. The solution for some—self-starvation—seems obvious, fatally so.

From these tragically extreme cases, it is not difficult to see the need to be perpetually dieting as a diluted form of sexual role rejection. Some men who find the overt sexuality of the mature woman threatening will encourage this behavior and reinforce the underlying anxiety. Those women who fail to make the effort to diet, for whatever reason, carry a burden of guilt for not striving to attain the slim silhouette we are all supposed to desire.

Too many women have lives that are tangled and tied by

these twin knots of guilt. One teaches us to reject our femininity and sexuality, the other traps us into self-rejection if we do
not conform to an ideal notion of how we should be. And there
we stay for decades, one part of the trap reinforcing the other,
while success eludes us because our motives are hidden by our
upbringing and our culture. We are neither free nor accepted.

Men who put on fat are almost equally rejected. With their
feminized bodies, they have difficulty finding partners—which
can be very distressing for the 25 percent of young men who are
overweight.

The background values of our culture magnify the pain inherent in this situation. If you are overweight, you are ugly,
and that is because you eat too much. You may not actually eat
a lot, but in terms of your own body, you are greedy, and that
as we all know is a very near cousin of the sin of gluttony. From
there the trap can be extended in almost any direction you
wish. Fat people are not only greedy, they are also obviously
lazy; they won't make the effort to balance input with output as
conventional wisdom says they should. It is all too easy to sur-
round fat with values that, in effect, destroy the lives of those
who are its victims. From uncertain sexuality, we can end up
with total self-rejection and destruction.

But, as we shall see later, many people caught in this trap of
values could be the victims of a serious misunderstanding of
the input/output equation because of the fourth function of fat.
The effect is to distort the role of fat in relation to the happy
fulfillment of our sexuality.

FAT AS INSULATION

We live in the temperate zone of the world. It goes without
saying that our climate is extremely variable and very fickle.
Our bodies have adapted by being able to put on fat quickly in
times of plenty, and to lose it slowly and cautiously as needed,
or when the summer returns. Fat was an essential part of our
survival repertoire, but today when life is not so harsh, this
ability is not appreciated.

If you are courageous enough to let your weight fluctuate as
it will over the course of a year, a logical pattern should emerge.

In the winter you will put on fat; then you'll lose it slowly as the days lengthen and the temperatures rise. Try on last summer's shorts in late spring and you may be distressed by those bulges above and below; if you resist the panic and carry on as though you didn't care, the chances are that by the hot days of summer, you'll look as good in them as you did last summer.

That spring blossoming of young women, so totally distracting to young men, is of course aided by the sudden revelation of previously covered winter fat.

In the late autumn, when the winds wake up, the days shorten, and temperatures fall, we miss the fat that floated away in those long, hot, summer days. The nagging desire for food intensifies; at times you feel you may blow away if you don't get some food inside you. If you are confident enough to respond to your body's needs, you will accept the hunger, eat, and put on weight as the weather turns colder. A little more fat will insulate your internal organs from the stress of the cold so that you can function more effectively, indoors as well as out.

Most of us do follow this natural pattern. Statistics on average calorie consumption—a guide to how much we eat, not to how much fat we put on—show that we eat most in the last three months of the year, and least from April to June.

Those who absolutely reject this natural cycle lose out in two ways. Fighting the body's desire for some winter fat is battling with all the inclinations of your metabolism. It is very stressful. Like all stress, it may have a variety of secondary health effects from raised blood pressure to reduced resistance to infections. You may keep off a few pounds, but you will risk paying a high price in health. And you will also be uncomfortable because you will feel the cold. You will be huddled up indoors, while your more realistic friends can enjoy the crisp air, perhaps skiing or taking part in other winter sports. If you give your body all the wrong messages, it will respond accordingly. It won't keep itself warm; it won't guard against infections as it should; and it certainly will not give you the energy you envy in others.

We are designed to cope with cold by putting on fat. A little more insulation tells our system everything is OK. And this need is not a superficial one that can be switched off by a fashionable diet, pill, or exercise routine. Northern races survived the last Ice Age because of this ability; it is not a lesson our genes will forget easily, nor will they let us forget it.

Indeed, many of us are so highly tuned to this response that a sudden drop in temperature during the day can push us toward the kitchen. Of course this urge will be increased for those who are already fighting off the fat, and may help tip them over the edge into a binge; it in turn will lead them into guilt and increased resolve, which will only make them more susceptible to another unintended binge. . . . It is a problem that can be easily avoided by a more understanding approach.

The long, thin body shape loses heat more efficiently. A more rounded body helps to conserve heat. This is because shorter, more rounded shapes have less surface area to radiate the heat. Although we can't alter the type of body we have, living in chilly conditions will tend to make us plumper than living in warmer climates. As those California girls should know, just living in a warm climate tends to keep you slim, whether you follow an esoteric fruit diet or not. And the same general rule is true for all of us, because the environment will have that effect on our basic nature.

An easy test to discover how fat acts as an insulator is to feel the different parts of your body in a cool room, say just before you get dressed. Your buttocks will feel relatively cold compared to your upper back, and other areas will show differences. Generally the effect is to insulate the core of your body, where all the vital organs are; the womb, of course, comes high on the list, so covering the bony girdle of the hips is a natural priority for the woman's body.

Recent research suggests that people with weight problems are not able to use fat for heating as effectively as do leaner people. Some scientists believe that they lack the special type of fat—brown adipose tissue or brown fat—that produces heat fastest. This may be because efforts to lose weight cause them to shed their most metabolically active stores of fat. The body seems to sacrifice cold-protection capacity by losing brown fat. This would explain why dieters often feel cold, even though they have obvious stores of insulating fat on their bodies, and why their metabolic processes are less likely to respond to sudden cold by burning fat.

FAT AS A FOOD STORE

Everyone knows that we store excess food as fat. In fact many people take it so much for granted that they imagine it to be the only function of fat. We believe we are right in putting it in third place.

The medical profession has consistently looked at fat in this way for the last century, which may explain the general ineffectiveness of doctors in dealing with problems of obesity and anorexia. They, along with the other "experts," state that, without question, fat develops as a result of the calorie equation being wrong; fat is a passive store of excessive input.

The reason for the persistence of this limited and narrow view is that it is partially true; the storage of excess food is one function of fat. But that is very different from saying, or behaving as if, calorie storage is the only function of fat.

If you are grossly overweight, it is quite possible that you could lose a lot of your excess by a simple calorie-control approach. Because, if you persistently eat more than you need, it will be stored as fat, and this store can in some cases be used up with little trouble. But you will find that the use of fat stores is subject to the law of diminishing returns. As you lose weight by calorie control, it becomes progressively harder to lose more weight by the same method.

Those who have tried to diet by calorie control alone will have discovered for themselves the very obvious and distressing limits of this view of fat. Even if you live for years on few calories, it is still possible to have a disproportionately large amount of fat on your body. So what are the realistic limits of this approach?

A store of fat in excess of that required for female contours and heat insulation is considered essential for the metabolism of women of reproductive years. Once more the inescapable logic of survival determines this tendency. If, having become attractive and shapely, you then become pregnant, your body wants to ensure that you have enough reserves to get you and the baby through nine months, which would have included at least part of a winter and the possibility of famine.

For women, during their reproductive years, the body will try to keep on a little extra fat as an insurance policy against damage to a possible baby. This protection will be maintained throughout adulthood. If for any reason this store gets too small, the hormones tend to diminish sexual desire. With further weight loss, menstruation will cease, ovulation will become erratic, and the chances of successful conception and pregnancy will be dramatically reduced.

So we have another paradox for the obsessive dieter who claims attraction of the opposite sex as her motivation. Are men really that easily fooled, or is she just fooling herself?

Most women will be in the traumatic hunger zone if they persistently try to reduce their calorie intake below the level at which their bodies can maintain adequate reserves to meet the needs of pregnancy. And if you and your body disagree on what is an adequate reserve, you face the misery of a lifelong battle with yourself—at least while you are capable of reproducing.

Dieting to below this fat level can be dangerous, because, in biological terms, reproduction is of primary importance. Essentially it amounts to this: if your body has to choose between your well-being and the survival of a child you might bear, the scales will tip in favor of your child. In practical terms, this means that, if you insist on losing weight below the level your body feels is right, you will not lose fat; you will lose lean tissue. This will be in the form of muscle, and also tissue from vital organs: your liver, kidneys, and heart. Your body will start to destroy you to protect your possible baby's chances. The pictures of unfortunate famine victims illustrate this; women who are obviously starving still have enough fat to maintain their breasts and feed their babies—these are the last systems to be shut down by starvation.

Over the decades many millions of women have subjected themselves to this destructive process, usually without realizing it. What they have observed is that after losing weight in this way, they tend to put fat on more rapidly than before. They are on the dieter's seesaw, where dieting actually makes them fat. With each rise in body weight, the proportion of fat increases. When their weight goes down, they tend to lose a greater proportion of lean tissue, and a classic vicious circle is set up. People who have been the victims of this are more likely to end up as sufferers of the PFR Syndrome, because the lean tissue lost may include essential liver tissue, which is one route into the syndrome. We will explain how and why later.

Before considering the final function of fat, it may be useful to summarize the points we have covered so far. We shall be breaking new ground, so it is a good idea to make sure that the old is in perspective before going on.

Fat, hated or not, is essential to body functions, particularly for women. It forms the body shape we recognize as typically feminine. It provides heat insulation, keeping our vital organs warm, and giving protection for babies. It also provides the body weight necessary for reproduction; women of reproductive age will be pushed to carry spare fuel in the form of fat to ensure their babies have the best chance of survival. Beyond this critical fat level, some surplus food may get put into store in the form of fat.

The reasons we have evolved to use fat in these ways are fairly straightforward. Fat is relatively inactive in metabolic terms; as you know it tends just to be there, so it does not require much energy for maintenance. The metabolic rate of people with high proportions of fat in their bodies is much lower than that of people with less fat and more muscle. This means that women, with higher fat proportions than men, need less food to keep them alive, and plumper women actually need less than their leaner sisters. And this is another factor that gives them, and their children, another edge for survival.

So the survival needs of our species drive us in a circle. Fat makes women distinctively female and signals their arrival at maturity. At some level, men understand that fat means better chances for the survival of their children and go along with the pattern reinforced by our evolutionary experience. So the daughters of women who use their fat effectively, for sexual attraction and survival, will tend to perpetuate the process. They carry the genes for a "thrifty" metabolism—one that will function effectively on little food—and they pass them on to their offspring. This is the essence of the survival of the fittest.

Our bodies are still very efficient at adapting to the conditions in which we live; the capacity to change in ways that will maximize our chances of survival is still there. Those adaptations we have been discussing which maximized the chances of our ancestors over millions of years of evolution still have a few tricks in reserve. While we as urban, well-clothed, well-heated, car-driving, and cared-for individuals, for whom food is always available, may not appreciate the effects of these survival tricks, we will not be able to control them unless we understand them.

At this point, before the emergence of the PFR Syndrome, it would have been possible to draw up a comprehensive strategy for almost anyone to lose as much weight as they wanted. Indeed, this is what we used to do for Life Profile clients, devising programs that would shed surplus food stores, then persuade the body it did not need pregnancy reserves or so much insulation.

It was the realization that fat had a fourth function that caused us to rewrite all our programs. We believe that all serious dieters need to drastically change their view of fat and its relationship to them, if they are to control their fat.

FAT AS A TOXIN STORE

We know what we mean by fat, but it is important to understand what we mean by a toxin. According to the *Concise Oxford Dictionary*, a toxin is "a poison, especially of animal or vegetable origin." As when trying to describe other new concepts, the existing definitions reveal their limitations. The PFR Syndrome is no exception. We have to extend the notion of a toxin to mean *any substance that the body treats as a poison*. It is the way in which the body treats toxins that holds the key to the problem of persistent fat retention.

As we have seen, the conventional view of fat is that it is essentially passive. It sits on the body, shaping, insulating, and storing food energy. What we are proposing is that fat also has an *active* role in the body: that of a storage medium for substances the body regards as toxic. When the body meets substances that are too toxic, or arriving too fast, to be broken down and excreted at the rate at which they are absorbed, they are put into storage. Different types of toxins enter tissues that are best suited to their storage. We know that lead is stored in bones, but the most common poisons we encounter today go into fat. Remember the clue of DDT in the fat of arctic seals?

We would go further. The problem of the PFR Syndrome is that the body will manufacture fat, in large quantities if necessary, and against all efforts to stop it, so that it can store toxins. The case histories in the next chapter illustrate this process quite clearly.

To see how this happens we need to understand how the body makes fat, and how it uses it up. It is the using-up process that is disrupted for large numbers of people, locking fat onto their bodies.

When we digest food it is broken down and rebuilt at the molecular level, rearranged into forms that we can use. Our digestive processes are complicated, but this has the advantage of allowing us to survive on almost anything. Our bodies rearrange the food molecules into the molecules it wants. We can even swap molecules around within our bodies, reusing them in different ways to meet different needs.

Carbohydrates, those foods many dieters traditionally, but erroneously, avoid, are broken down into sugars, fiber, and other constituents. The sugars and valuable trace components are absorbed, while the indigestible carbohydrates, which we call fiber, continue to move through the intestines. Proteins, larger and even more complex molecules, are split into smaller molecules called polypeptides, and later into their constituent amino acids—the basic building blocks of life. Fats are broken down to fatty acids and glycerol; fatty acids may be used in various metabolic processes, while glycerol is changed by the liver's enzyme systems into glucose. This can be stored in the liver in the form of glycogen or released into the bloodstream for instant energy.

The liver is the real "backroom" of our body. It does not usually get much publicity or attention, but it should. It performs over twenty major functions, all essential for our well-being. The best way to think of the liver is as a vast warehouse, with trucks constantly coming in and being reconnected to take trailers to different destinations. Some traffic will go off and come in by other means: rail or water. The whole system is integrated by communications at many levels, signals, sensors, and a computer.

All our digested food moves around the body in our blood. From the digestive organs, it is carried directly into the liver by the hepatic portal vein, the main input to the warehouse where the sorting begins. Now, in addition to all our nutrients, the blood will also be carrying substances we don't want. The liver metabolizes, or breaks down for disposal, such substances; they may range from cancer cells, viruses, the natural products of cellular breakdown, hormones, and fat being recycled for energy, to drugs and other foreign substances.

The most common exit route for unwanted substances is through our kidneys. But the substances have to be made soluble in water before they can be shipped out this way. For those that cannot be dissolved in water, the next choice is to dissolve them in fat. They are carried in the bile, which is secreted by the liver, into the bile duct and then into the digestive tract once more. If they take the hint, these substances are eliminated as solid waste. Unfortunately this system is not very efficient. To save effort, the endlessly busy liver recycles bile, losing only small amounts as waste, and inevitably some of the garbage gets recycled as well; this is the messy end of the process. There is some advantage in this disorder. More or less constant levels of some substances can be maintained by recirculating; other substances can be recycled, thus saving effort for other systems. The danger is that substances that are totally undesirable are not totally eliminated, and they can build up in the system.

When the liver can't cope, fat-soluble substances go into storage to be dealt with later. They are stored in body fat. The substances that overload the liver will vary from individual to individual. They may range from known poisons and drugs to food additives. But they will tend to have one thing in common: they are most likely to be the ubiquitous, man-made, organic molecules that are increasingly common in the twentieth-century environment.

When the system becomes overloaded, or its capacity is reduced, an increasing number of substances are likely to be shunted into fat. Whether the liver will be able to cope at a later time is then the crucial question. In the meantime, the result is the deposit of Toxic Adipose Tissue—TAT, or contaminated fat.

Perhaps we should not be surprised that substances the liver can't cope with end up in deposits of fat. The low turnover of tissue reflected in fat's inherently slow metabolic rate means that any poisons stored in fat can be left undisturbed where they will do the least harm. In most parts of the body there is a constant cycle of breakdown and renewal; for example, it is estimated that we replace all the bones of our skeleton every seven years. In fat there is little activity. It is accumulated, and there it stays until it is broken down for energy. Its insulating and shaping properties are entirely passive; it could be replaced by a wrap of foam or a pad of silicon.

There are other characteristics that make fat ideal for toxin storage. As many of us know, it can be put on very quickly, frighteningly fast at times. And it can be put on in large amounts. Because it has a low metabolic rate, it does not require much in the way of auxiliary servicing—no ligaments, bones, very few nerves, hardly any major blood vessels. The fat cells are there ready to be filled up as required.

Of course this will not be everyone's experience. The easy deposition of persistent fat will come as news to some. They are the lucky ones. People do vary enormously in many ways, both obviously and very subtly. For some, toxins will be much more readily neutralized by their metabolic processes. Indeed, the old saying dear to grandmother, that one man's meat is another man's poison, was correct—one woman's harmless substances may be another's forty-pound weight gain. The "lucky" ones, confronted with the same substances, will not produce the same stores of fat because they don't need them.

But there are others who are simply not as efficient at dealing with toxins. This may be because of the way they live, or because of liver damage, or simply because they started out with a relatively small liver in relation to their body weight. For these individuals, persistent fat retention can take another step; the toxins they cannot cope with will actually damage their livers, thus further reducing their capacity to cope with toxins.

For those who have been on the diet seesaw, losing lean tissue in favor of fat with each up-and-down of weight, the loss of liver tissue may be crucial. Their decreased metabolic capacity will make it even more likely that the body will put on fat—and lock it up with toxins it cannot deal with. If they persist in dieting, their livers will become even less efficient because their limited stores of a crucial detoxifying substance (glutathione— its role is described in detail in Chapter 15) are used up in the effort to maintain the function of the rest of the body.

With decreased coping capacity, the metabolism comes to regard more substances as toxic. This is what happens with increasing age; metabolic shocks that we could bounce through or over in the vitality of youth can put us in bed for a few days. Under some circumstances, if metabolic capacity continues to decrease, there is a point of no return; the unfortunate alcoholic who dies of cirrhosis of the liver is the most familiar example.

We are not suggesting that persistent fat is a sign of imminent death. What we are saying is this: you may be subjecting your systems to a range of subtle influences that have the combined effect of creating a toxic reaction. The protective response of the body to this toxic reaction is to lay down fat to store the toxin. Until you put on the fat, and find you can't shift it, you may not notice anything at all—because this coping mechanism allows you to stay healthy, in spite of exposure to high levels of toxic substances.

The changes that make you susceptible to PFR are often not obvious. The exception may be when there is an obvious response to marked changes in environmental conditions. Answering the question of why so many thin women suddenly put on weight was difficult because of the subtle and varying causes of the condition.

The process is easier to understand if we accept that fat has a lot to do with our ability to survive, and that this ability has been extended recently to include acting as an active storage medium for harmful toxins. These women's bodies were acting in the best way they could to protect them from a serious hazard.

Our bodies tend to overdo it, to err on the side of safety. The problem of staying thin is to persuade our bodies that enough is enough, and perhaps a little less than enough would be quite adequate. For the first three functions of fat, persuasion is the only successful tactic; for the fourth, once we have become victims of the PFR Syndrome, the only answer is detoxification. Our strategy explains how to do this.

Perhaps, in conclusion, we should consider how widespread the PFR Syndrome is. We cannot be sure of figures, of course; your individual experience in your own case is the best indicator of your position. But we are left wondering if we may not have stumbled across the answer to that large puzzle: could it be that the reason why as a nation we are eating less and less, yet weighing more and more, is that to some degree we are all victims of this syndrome? That our bodies are being called upon to cope with ever more toxins, and that increased weight in the form of fat is the body's only answer to this chemical onslaught?

5

The PFR Syndrome

The PFR Syndrome is the effect of toxins on body fat. The human body is capable of dissolving a great range of potentially poisonous substances in fat, and of producing fat to store these substances. Toxins that can induce this reaction are very widespread in our environment; we absorb them in our food and from many other sources. The fat becomes poisoned in the process, and once it is poisoned it is very difficult to shift. PFR victims are people who carry excess weight that they find they cannot lose. Their bodies retain stores of persistent fat.

The clearest sign of the PFR Syndrome is a sudden increase in fatty tissue. In this context, "sudden" may mean a few weeks or a period of months. The latter is more likely, if you have been consistently trying to lose weight while your body has been trying to put it on.

If you have recently put on weight and now find it will not shift, even though you may have put it on and taken it off quite easily in the past, it is almost certainly a case of PFR. In addition to obvious fat, cellulite and that less dense, "watery" flab—typically hanging from the upper arms and thighs—may also be used by the body to store toxic residues. PFR Syndrome victims have bodies that create deposits of toxic adipose tissue in a variety of sites. All forms of such tissue can be reduced by the same treatment.

28

Have you, before or during a period of weight gain, been exposed to anything in your environment which your body may regard as toxic? It may be that, in the absence of any direct and sudden exposure, your system is responding adversely to a low-level buildup over a long time. This is particularly likely if you've been dieting or been sick.

Some drugs are known to cause weight gain. If you have recently taken medication for a particular problem, say depression, and found yourself putting on unexplained weight, that is characteristic of the PFR Syndrome. Similarly, taking oral contraceptives will make you more susceptible to it. A wide range of other substances have been noted as causal factors, but because of individual variability, it is impossible to give a comprehensive checklist. At the end of this chapter, you will find a broad guide to possible causes, but remember that your experience after use of, or exposure to, a particular substance is the best guide to any effects on you.

One effect that may be noticeable after exposure to a toxin is an unusual desire for sweet or fatty foods. Your body may be demanding those substances that can be directly routed into fat stores. It can be an indication that your liver needs to dump something it cannot deal with into fat.

Other signs of toxic exposure that may lead to persistent fat retention include rashes, brittle nails, and unusual shedding of hair. These can mean that the body is struggling to get rid of substances it does not like. Rashes may be the immune system working to shed matter through the skin, while nail and hair growth require proteins related to those urgently needed by the liver for detoxification.

The role of the liver is crucial in the PFR Syndrome. Small people will tend to be more at risk, simply because they have smaller livers. A rough guide to the efficiency of your liver is the effect alcohol has on you. Some victims have reported getting drunk on one or two small drinks, and getting a nasty hangover from one more. Obviously, their livers were not coping too well. Other signs are that physical effort tends to produce a "hangover" effect some time later. Or you may feel cold while others seem comfortable.

Similarly, people who have some other condition, such as an

allergy, which indicates a malfunction of the immune system or the liver metabolism, will be more at risk. This group includes those who suffer from arthritis and other autoimmune diseases, as well as hayfever, asthma, eczema, and food allergy sufferers. The Plan we suggest will help (see page 69), both by reducing susceptibility to such conditions and by reducing the risk of PFR.

Lastly we must consider those people who have been fat for years, and may have given up hope of getting that weight off. For many women the extra weight is associated with having children. From the attractive person they were before pregnancy, too often they develop a matronly shape that they would rather not have. It is usually assumed that the change in routine associated with being a mother is the cause of this change— but is it? If they have been depriving themselves of food in a long-term effort to control the weight gain, they will be more at risk because they will have been interfering with their detoxifying systems.

During pregnancy, the liver and kidneys, as well as everything else, work for two. This in itself is a strain, but one we are designed to cope with. If you add to it environmental toxins, however, you could be on the edge of a PFR problem. The final factor that may tip pregnant women over the edge is the range of drugs they may be given during the actual birth. Anesthetics are particularly troublesome for our metabolism, and in an already overloaded state, they could be the last straw. For some women, each successive pregnancy adds to the problem. Of course this same route might apply to other operations—one of our mothers has been chubby ever since a hysterectomy.

So you should consider your medical history for the start of any undesirable long-term trends.

It may be that you are one of those people who can lose most of their fat by either diet or exercise, but find that whatever they do, a particular lump will not shift. A common PFR pattern in these cases is that people become thin all over—except for a layer of fat on their bellies. It can occur in other parts of the body; it depends on the distribution of your most reactive fat cells.

Similarly, you may find that you can lose fat, but only up to a certain point. You need to decide what sort of fat your body is hanging on to, and why. Could it be toxic adipose tissue? Only you can decide. Check where your body prefers to lose it from: if you are losing sexual shaping, from breasts and hips, while keeping fat elsewhere, this is probably PFR.

If your attempts at dieting or physical activity produce headaches or "hangovers," beware. This means that the toxins you have stored in fat are coming back to haunt you. You are a PFR victim and should follow The Plan. Apart from joint aches and pains, and muscular stiffness from unaccustomed effort, physical activity should not produce effects of this sort. If you experience "hangovers," and are at all unsure about the cause, it would be advisable to check with your physician to eliminate other possibilities, but in most cases the answer will be obvious.

Finally, erratic fat loss may be your best overall guide. The diagram below indicates how your body should shed fat. Only you can decide how much fat you have, or need, for each function. If your body does not lose weight in the way indicated, it is because it is expressing some desire to retain fat to protect itself. You then have to remove the need for that protection. The PFR escape plan will tell you how to do this.

CHECKLIST

The following factors may make you relatively more susceptible to the PFR Syndrome:

1. Female gender

2. Short stature

3. Repeated pregnancies

4. Present or past use of oral contraceptives

5. Use of hormone replacement therapy

6. Use of medication (see Appendix 2)

7. Cigarette smoking

8. Heavy drinking

9. Sensitivity to alcohol or solvents

10. Symptoms of allergy, such as hayfever, eczema, perennial rhinitis (chronic runny nose), allergic asthma, food intolerance

11. Exposure to heavy environmental pollution—through city living, living close to petrochemical factories or similar industry, exposure to fumes in workplace

12. Poor nutrition

13. Emotional stress

14. Inactivity

15. Poor circulation

The following signs may be associated with a PFR problem:

1. Rashes

2. Brittle fingernails

3. Unusual hair loss

4. Dull, unhealthy-looking skin and hair

5. Autoimmune disease, including arthritis, nephritis, ulcerative colitis

NOTES

You should not try to lose fat other than in the order indicated. Although you might lose weight, you would create an unnatural body shape, and persisting with misguided efforts could put your health at risk.

1. To diet successfully, you must first remove toxic adipose tissue. If you do not, it will persist even when you have lost all other fat, and it will hinder your efforts to lose weight however you go about it. Once you have got rid of it, you will be able to

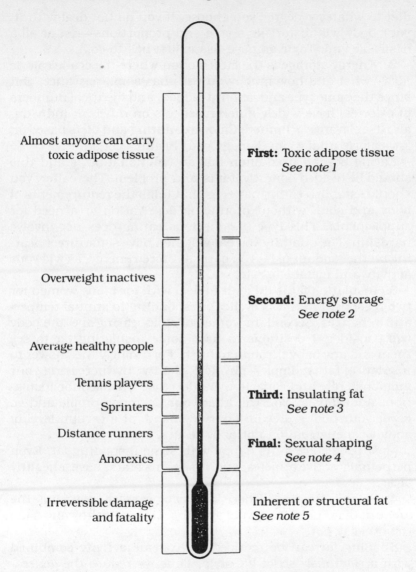

Almost anyone can carry
toxic adipose tissue

First: Toxic adipose tissue
See note 1

Overweight inactives

Second: Energy storage
See note 2

Average healthy people

Tennis players

Sprinters

Third: Insulating fat
See note 3

Distance runners

Anorexics

Final: Sexual shaping
See note 4

Irreversible damage
and fatality

Inherent or structural fat
See note 5

diet to whatever degree you choose. If you do not deal with it, your body will distort its shape and proportions—not at all a desirable end. Toxic adipose tissue just has to go.

2. Energy storage is the fat function where the crude calorie idea—what and how much you eat—has some relevance. But since the same type and amount of food, and identical numbers of calories, have widely different effects on different individuals, its relevance is limited. Calorie counting and diets based on low-calorie intake can damage your health.

Eating beyond need often has an emotional basis and this should be tackled honestly if it is your problem. Thereafter, you should establish eating patterns that fulfill the requirements of body and soul, without producing deprivation or a need for supplements. This type of conscious eating does not involve hardship. The quantity you eat will then have some direct bearing on the amount of fat you carry as stored energy, as will your activity and metabolic rate.

3. Insulating fat is difficult to deal with for many women for two reasons. First, it is cyclical, responding to annual temperature changes. Second, in women of childbearing age, the body will consider it desirable to have some insulating fat to see them and any baby through to birth. Fortunately the answer to insulating fat is simple—physical activity. By increasing your metabolic rate and capacity, you decrease the need for insulation. Additionally, you will alter your hormone profile and so lower your body's precautionary demand; at a certain level of activity, menstruation normally ceases.

Most people are quite happy with some insulating fat. Even perpetually active athletes, such as tennis stars, have a healthy layer.

4. Sexual shaping. There are two ways of reducing the amount of fat used for sexual shaping. One is healthy and safe; the other is not.

Shaping fat can be reduced by extreme activity combined with a rigorously strict life-style. Thus we reduce the generation of fat by matching input to output in energy terms, and by altering the body's hormone profile to the degree that it is convinced that such fat is of minimal importance. When activity decreases and the life-style is relaxed, the body will put on this fat once more. Because of the highly active life-style, this way of losing fat is usually without risk; such individuals are extremely fit. It is rare, however; even world-class runners like Mary Decker Slaney have some minimal feminine shaping from their fat.

Sexual shaping can also be reduced by starvation, by metabolic changes, by psychological suffering, or by a combination of these factors, as in anorexia nervosa. Losing weight in any of these ways is not healthy; people who do so are clinically ill.

5. Extreme efforts to lose fat eventually damage those parts of the body that require fatty tissue for their function—for example, the nervous system and brain. Such misguided efforts can prove fatal.

6

Case Histories

On her wedding day Amanda Phillips was as thin and pretty as any young woman could wish to be. She was small and delicately built, and her weight had remained stable at 98 pounds for almost ten years—ever since her early teens. Unlike many less fortunate women, she had not had to struggle to achieve this happy state. Staying thin had never been a problem for her; she had no trouble with her appetite, no nagging hunger. And she had always enjoyed energetic sports. She was the sort of person we think of envyingly as naturally thin and active.

After Amanda had been married for less than a year, she became unaccountably depressed. Looking back now on those black months she still cannot understand what set it all off. We can only speculate: the change in life-style associated with marriage, an accumulation of small stresses, or perhaps a bad reaction to something in her environment.

Like so many experiencing a sudden and apparently inexplicable change, Amanda consulted her doctor. He could not pin down her problem, but accepted her weepy and miserable symptoms at face value. He took the only action that seemed open to him and prescribed antidepressant drugs. Amanda took them gratefully.

Her deep depression did not lift immediately, but the doctor explained that the pills often had a delayed effect, and she persisted with the treatment. Gradually her mood changed for the better. In relief at the prospect of returning to her normal, happy self, Amanda overlooked the other changes that were happening to her. She now felt ravenously hungry all the time and found herself desiring the sort of foods that had never appealed to her before. Suddenly cakes, cookies, and candy seemed irresistible.

The doctor was reassuring; he explained that an increased appetite was generally considered a healthy sign, probably the consequence of her improved mood. Just as she had lost interest in food during her depression, lifting the depression was almost bound to have the opposite effect. He agreed that she might put on weight, but suggested that this was a small price for the improvement, and she would soon lose it again once her depression was completely cured.

Amanda's delicate, girlish figure soon showed the effects, but she and her husband disguised any anxiety by buying new clothes to celebrate her improvement. However, the problem grew too great to ignore; in a few months Amanda had put on 42 pounds.

The excess weight, so quickly gained, proved impossible to lose. Try as she might, Amanda could not rid herself of the fat belly that she had acquired. At first people smiled, assuming she was pregnant. But as the months passed, and she still looked six months pregnant, it became obvious that this was not the case. The change and the embarrassment it caused destroyed her social life.

With the information you already have, what had happened to Amanda may appear obvious. But, at the end of the 1970s when this was happening to her, the fourth function of fat, the problem of toxic adipose tissue producing the PFR Syndrome, was simply not suspected. Many pieces of the puzzle were on the table, but nobody had put them together.

Being the sort of person she is, Amanda did not accept her situation. Her first attempts to shift her fat were through dieting. Over a two-year period she tried every diet she could find, and her food intake declined to less than a thousand calories a day. Yet the fat persisted.

She also tried to return to her previous activity level. But this proved impossible. She was simply unable to summon the energy to make it work. The least exertion made her feel desperately tired. She could still swim, but her embarrassment at her comical appearance in a swimsuit made the public pool more than she could face. Finally even walking made her feel tired.

Her determination survived, however. Amanda tried exercising in the privacy of her home. She bought aerobics books and tapes and faithfully followed the exercises, keeping the promise they held firmly in mind. She jogged and twisted to the music of the beginners' routine until sweat ran into her eyes. Gritting her teeth, she fought the desire to drop onto the sofa.

Next day Amanda stayed in bed. She had never felt so ill in her life before. Her head hammered relentlessly; she was weak and felt sick; and her lack of coordination made standing up difficult. It was as though the previous day's exercise had given her an almighty hangover. A week later, when she had recovered, she tried again with the same result. Another week later, Amanda tried a little jogging—only to find it gave her a severe headache.

The effort hangover is a common symptom of the PFR Syndrome. Amanda's experience is a more dramatic form of Hetty Einzig's feeling, described in *Dieting Makes You Fat*, that by running she had been releasing poisons into her system. Although it may seem to rule out activity because of its unpleasant effects, as we will see later, this reaction among victims can be used as a part of The Plan to beat the syndrome.

It was around this time that Amanda contacted Life Profile and stimulated our search for the answer to her problem. Amanda expressed a strong suspicion about the cause of her weight problem; she blamed the antidepressant drugs her doctor had given her. She also reported that she had consulted a variety of specialists, who dismissed her suggestion. While they conceded that perhaps antidepressants might cause some temporary weight gain, their opinion was that this weight would come off again. One suggested that Amanda stay in a hospital for a week on a monitored diet; he obviously did not believe that she was eating as little as she claimed.

Amanda had tried all the conventional means of losing her

excess weight, yet it would not shift. Clearly some mechanism was binding that unwanted fat to her body in a way that had not previously been suspected. Solving the way this mechanism might work was the problem we were confronted with; if we could discover what was going on, the hope was that it could be reversed.

We started by taking her suspicion seriously and consulting the medical information on antidepressant drugs. The literature on these drugs does note weight gain as a common side effect. It is an effect that has been investigated by psychiatrists, some of whom perceptively observed that this supposedly minor reaction was capable of making its victims even more depressed than they were before they started the drug therapy. For those who already felt unhappy because they were overweight and unattractive, this sort of side effect could be enough to tip them toward desperation and even suicide. It is far from a minor or trivial reaction to drug treatment in such cases.

We could not find any explanation in the medical literature for Amanda's reaction, or for the fact that the fat she had put on was so persistent. Meanwhile, the search of Life Profile records produced some other cases, which, although not as extreme, had some things in common with Amanda's experience.

The next part of the puzzle was provided by Beth Jackson. Unlike Amanda, Beth had been fighting a tendency to put on weight ever since her teens. She knew that if she wasn't active, if she didn't watch what she ate, she would put on weight. Once this happened, she would deliberately change her habits, perhaps starve herself a bit, so that the unwanted weight disappeared again. As she got into her mid-twenties, Beth found that if she put on weight, she had to diet conscientiously and be very active to get it off. She also found that it seemed to go on again with increased ease.

Although it was annoying to have to devote more time and effort to weight control, Beth accepted this as part of the life of a career woman. Over nearly a decade she was able to keep on top of it without too much difficulty, providing nothing threw her off balance. But, without realizing it, Beth was on the diet seesaw. Each time she shed weight, she was losing a little more lean tissue, and each time she put on weight she had a higher proportion of fat.

What finally threw Beth was lifting a box of paper in the office. Trouble with a disk in her spine put her on her back in bed for three weeks. During this period, she was taking pills for the pain in her recovering back, and, perhaps out of frustration, she was drinking a lot more than usual. Under these conditions she put on weight very quickly.

When she recovered, Beth went back to her old diet and activity routine. It had always worked for her before, after holidays, or when she had got into the habit of eating and drinking for comfort after the breakup of a love affair. This time her routine failed her. For all her efforts, Beth was unable to shift more than a very small amount of the weight she had put on during the months of trouble with her back.

For a long time, Beth assumed that the reason for her problem had simply been her reduced level of activity. But this explanation didn't make a lot of sense. Why was it, she wondered, that the weight stayed on in spite of a sensible diet and a regular exercise routine? This had never happened to her before, and now, at thirty-three, although she knew she was not experiencing any major metabolic change, she wondered if it might be just her age. But a nagging doubt remained. It just didn't feel right.

We looked in detail at Beth's activity and diet habits, and naturally we followed up the drugs she had been taking during her back episode. These were nonsteroidal anti-inflammatories, of which there are many forms. Their main use is the reduction of chronic pain. There was no general acknowledgment that they caused weight gain, although weight gain is common among those who take this type of drug on a regular basis, and it is noted as a side effect for some members of the group.

It is usually assumed that any weight gain is associated with inactivity caused by the painful conditions for which such drugs are prescribed. Arthritis is the most common reason for such long-term use, and by and large this seemed to be a reasonable explanation for most weight gain associated with these drugs.

We were left wondering whether there might not be a little over-simplification in this explanation, like the explanation that those who grew fat on antidepressants did so because their improved mood led them to eat more. While we could understand people putting on weight when their arthritis interfered with their mobility, what of those whose problems were with their hands? Why should they tend to grow fat too?

It was Beth's drinking that focused our investigation. Not that she drank a lot; most of the time she drank hardly at all, but like most of us she would, every now and then, indulge. She had done so at the time she was taking drugs for her back problem. This caused us to focus on what might have been happening in her liver at this time. It was a significant step toward discovering the PFR mechanism.

Christopher Denham's weight problem coincided with the onset of asthma. He had been a small, rather delicate child, susceptible to allergic problems, though these had been comparatively minor. The onset of asthma during early adulthood came as a frightening new development when he and his family moved into the country. He believes the onset was prompted by the accidental drift of pesticide from aerial spraying into his garden.

Chris had discovered that when his asthma was mild, as it was when he lived in Spain, he had little trouble with his weight. But in periods when he was having more frequent or severe attacks, he would put on weight at an alarming rate. When his asthma was controlled with sodium chromoglycate, the problem of weight gain persisted.

We know that many allergic problems, such as hayfever, are basically caused by pollution. Not necessarily the pollution that we acknowledge—the dirt, litter, smoke, and fumes that are so offensive—but also the myriad "safe" chemical products which are so common in our modern world. Most of these artificial substances are those organic molecules that the liver stores in fat. Was Chris's case giving us a direct clue? If pollution (with the sudden overload of pesticide, a type of chemical absolutely consistent with both allergic reaction and fat deposition) precipitated his asthma, might it not also be linked to his weight cycles?

We were almost convinced.

Donna had struggled with weight and fitness throughout her teens and early twenties. Her Life Profile course had enabled her to achieve stable weight and an active life, and she and her husband were happily working to set themselves up before starting a family.

Then suddenly she put on weight very rapidly. Like some other apparently stable clients, she had lost balance. We were trying to solve these clients' problems on an individual basis, assuming that there was no common thread, when we began to consider the possibility of the PFR Syndrome.

Donna's rapid weight gain was triggered by causes that we subsequently recognized in other cases: exposure to a different environment with a particular range of new chemical hazards. Donna started work in an electrical parts factory. Industry has become reliant on the use of new synthetic materials; the electrical industry uses them to coat wires for insulation, to make boards for printed circuits, and for a wide range of other processes. During manufacturing, quantities of these materials are released into the atmosphere, to be breathed in or absorbed through the skin.

The common experience in our cases had now emerged. They had all been exposed to one or more toxic substances. Just how this precipitated their PFR Syndrome is the subject of the next chapter.

7

PFR—The Cause

PFR is caused by exposure to toxic substances that are dumped by the victim's metabolism into toxic adipose tissue.

To justify this conclusion we have to go back to our earlier definition of a toxic substance as *any substance that the body treats as a poison.*

In the cases described in the previous chapter, the victims had been exposed to toxic substances in quantities greater than their metabolic processes could deal with. Their bodies had reacted by dumping the excess into fat, laying down more fat to store these toxins safely. This fat was then protected and maintained by the body, so that it persisted despite all efforts to shift it. Ridding the body of this fat would mean flooding the system with toxins once more.

This statement may surprise some readers. What toxic substance had Amanda been exposed to? She had become depressed, was prescribed drug therapy, and had put on weight. Where do toxins figure in this case?

Most people do not think of medicines as poisons. We are accustomed to focusing only on their beneficial effects. We forget that there is no such thing as a safe drug; it is easy to overlook the fact that drugs are almost always chemicals which are foreign to the human body, and are at the least regarded as suspicious substances by our metabolic processes. Pharmacologists, who study drugs, and toxicologists, who study poisons, agree that drugs are poisons administered in small doses. All drugs are capable of causing damage to the human body. The quantity that the body will accept without protest or signs of poisoning will vary, from one substance to another, and from one individual to another.

So a normal therapeutic dose of any medicine may prove entirely beneficial to one person—yet life-threatening to another. Fortunately the latter response is rare. The testing carried out is intended to reduce the frequency of such events. Nevertheless, even the safest drugs do kill people and cause a wide variety of unwanted adverse reactions or side effects. Amanda was a victim of one of these adverse reactions.

Amanda's antidepressant drugs did not make her ill because, although her systems were clearly not coping well enough for the drug to be harmlessly eliminated, a second line of defense had come into operation. Her body had manufactured stores of fat where the potentially damaging substance, or more likely, derivatives from its partial metabolization, had been dumped. This would protect the other organs of her body, such as her heart, from exposure to an overdose.

Her PFR resulted from the fact that any attempt to use that fat would put the toxic drug derivatives back into circulation. Her body would then react in exactly the same way it did the first time it was exposed to these substances—and put them straight back into fat. It seemed that whatever she did, that fat was firmly locked to her body. The "hangovers" she experienced with exercise were just that—hangovers caused by the toxins in her circulation affecting other organs of her body. She recovered when most of the toxin was back in fat stores once more.

Beth's problem is less clear-cut. Inactivity, anti-inflammatory drugs, and alcohol all contributed. On the face of it, inactivity caused by her back problem seems the obvious culprit. But that does not explain why the weight would not come off again. Her PFR was the result of a pattern of events which at a particular point in her life, under particular circumstances, produced this effect. Her seesaw dieting over the years had probably reduced the capacity of her liver through lean-tissue loss. Then combining drugs and alcohol overloaded her detoxification system. Had she been her normal, active self, her system might have coped, but being flat on her back could have been the last straw—her body chose to store its overload in fat.

It is impossible to be absolutely sure, but this interpretation seems to fit all the facts. Though why the body should choose to continue with this option once she became active again is not clear. Whatever the precise route to the problem, there is no denying that Beth became a sufferer of the PFR Syndrome.

In Amanda's case the nature of the substance involved probably caused her fat to lock up. With Beth another mechanism may have come into operation. It reveals another source of the PFR problem: if anything lowers our capacity to detoxify, or subjects it to a temporary overload, our metabolism can switch to a different coping system. Clearly, if a variety of factors are priming it and pushing it toward switching, the nature of the last straw involved becomes less critical and consequently more difficult to identify. We will look at a wider range of potential priming factors for the PFR Syndrome later.

Beth's metabolic switch shows the danger of overload caused by a range of potential toxins interacting with life-style factors. It is almost as if the metabolism learns a new trick and then finds it preferable to the old—a very human reaction after all! But this is only a guess; few processes in the body can be explained by a single mechanism, working in one way, and in apparent isolation. Usually a combination of things are at work at many levels to produce the effects we become aware of. This flexibility is a part of the wonder of our being.

Similarly, the reason for unusual sensitivity to the side effects of drugs is often unknown. It is generally assumed that it has to do with variations in the efficiency and balance of enzyme systems that are involved in detoxification. This brings us back to the liver, where these enzymes are produced and do their work, rearranging and disposing of the substances involved. If the systems in a person's body are unable to deal with drugs or other substances, as soon as they arrive at the liver, then the quantities build up. Eventually they will reach toxic levels.

Christopher's susceptibility to allergic problems was established before he was exposed to the particular episode that apparently precipitated his asthma. It happened to be exposure to large amounts of pesticide in the air, but it could equally well have been any one of a wide range of substances now circulating in our environment. The substances that overload a person to the point where allergies such as eczema, hayfever, and asthma are triggered are numerous and widespread. This is why these conditions are increasingly common. Billions of gallons of pesticides are now sprayed onto our land and food each year and are frequently associated with this sort of reaction. Environmental groups have numerous reports of case histories of such individuals.

The essence of an allergic reaction is that the body treats a substance that it may have previously regarded as safe, as dangerous or poisonous. This change of reaction may occur at many levels, involving both the immune and detoxification systems. In hayfever sufferers, the mast cells—the gatekeepers of the immune system—which line membranes exposed to the air, confuse harmless pollen grains with dangerous organisms; while similar mast cells in the digestive system of food-allergy sufferers misidentify food components as poisonous.

The general feature of allergic conditions is that common substances, which are harmless to the majority of people, are treated as poisonous by the sufferer's system. The immune and detoxification systems of the body can become stretched in dealing both with these pseudo-poisons and with the treatments taken to counter their effects.

Allergy itself can cause weight gain in some sufferers. Clinical ecologist Richard Mackarness has commented that a cereal-free diet developed for weight loss, which worked in spite of the fact that it was not low in calories, produced its effects through the elimination from the diet of substances that provoked allergy.

Another clue to the PFR mechanism was reported in *Eating Dangerously* by Richard Mackarness. He recounts the experience of Dr. Pennington, who was given the task of developing a weight-reducing plan for executives of the Du Pont chemical company. He "came to the conclusion that obesity in some people is caused by an inability to use carbohydrates for anything except making surplus fat. He . . . postulated a shortcut into the fat stores with subsequent difficulty in getting the fat out again for conversion into energy." Even if one ignores the irony that the victims were employees of a chemical company, it is obvious that Dr. Pennington was bumping into the PFR Syndrome without recognizing it. As also, we believe, was Dr. Mackarness.

For those whose route into the PFR Syndrome is through an allergic reaction, it makes no difference whether we would recognize the substance they are allergic to as a toxin or not. What is important is that their body believes the substance to be toxic and then decides to dump it, "making surplus fat" to contain it.

In the conventional treatment of allergic reactions, the drug route can once more be implicated in PFR. Most of the drugs used to treat allergies are known to cause weight gain in some who take them, although this may not tip over into PFR. The most effective—and the most dangerous—drugs used for allergy treatment are steroids. Long-term use can produce a characteristic accumulation of fat in the "dowager's hump" on the upper back. Fat is also laid down on the trunk and the face; those who take steroids for long periods are characterized by their round "moon" faces.

Antihistamines, the most commonly used drugs for allergic problems, can induce weight gain. They may also have the effect of depressing the immune system, thus making some people more vulnerable to both infections and toxins. Some of the newer types, free from the side effect of drowsiness common with the older forms, have nevertheless been observed to cause weight gain in some users.

Our conclusion is that anyone who is susceptible to allergic reactions is at an increased risk of developing PFR. Such a person's system is juggling at various levels with substances it does not like; what action it will take if it should fail, or if it has to cope with more, is unpredictable; but PFR is an obvious safety net.

We have now to consider the wider causes of PFR, the sources of overload of the systems we have been discussing. Drugs, which our bodies treat as toxic, are taken usually through choice, and we can control this source. But we are all taking in substances, both acknowledged poisons and others considered "safe," all the time. We are all to some degree poisoned without being aware of it.

Everyone in the Western world now carries some poisoned fat on their body. Indeed, it may be true that everyone in the world is contaminated. This is because the sort of substances which migrate easily into fat are everywhere in our environment. The example of DDT illustrates how they can affect us.

DDT (dichlorodiphenyltrichloroethane) is, or rather was, a highly effective pesticide. It was widely used against everything from body lice and flies to mosquitoes in countrywide antimalarial campaigns. Over the last four decades millions of tons have been released into the environment. The chemical is very biospecific—it has a marked affinity for living organisms—and it is lethal to many pest species . . . until they acquire immunity.

The problem is that DDT is not biodegradable. In fact it is rather the opposite, a molecule that combines its biospecific qualities with a very high motivation, working hard to incorporate itself into living matter. It is almost as if it were working its way up the food chain, away from those insects that are now immune to it, into more complex animals, who find it more difficult to deal with. Could this molecule's aim be to become an essential component of living cells? This idea is not really fantastic; all the organic molecules now incorporated in the lifeforms of our biosphere must have moved up in this way during the evolution of life. The question at the back of our minds should be, how many of the thousands of biospecific molecules we now use have the same properties?

Studies of the chemical composition of human fat reveal that all of us carry residues of DDT, dieldrin, and other persistent organic insecticides. These were once used widely and thoughtlessly—they still are in some parts of the world.

Our tissues are also saturated with metabolites of food additives. Preservatives, for example, do not only preserve the meat we eat; but also linger in our flesh with the same effect. Both American and British undertakers have reported that corpses actually stay fresh for two to three weeks longer than they ever used to!

We take in these toxic substances with our food, in the air we breathe, and we absorb them through our skin. Exactly what happens to them depends on our individual metabolism, susceptibility, and the nature and quantity of the substances to which we are exposed. Different forms of potential poison also interact with one another to further complicate any predictions we might try to make about their effects.

This terrible complexity means in effect that we are gambling with our bodies all the time. We cannot hope to predict or understand completely all that is going on. Nevertheless, some general principles are quite clear. Fat deposition is most likely to occur when we are exposed to substances our bodies treat as poisonous, and when these substances are readily soluble in fat.

The most important of these are organic compounds based on carbon-ring systems. All life on this planet is based upon molecules assembled around carbon atoms, and the artificial molecules manufactured by industrial chemists are based on the hydrocarbon-ring systems found in oil and coal—this is why such products are termed "organic." The substances produced around these molecular rings are few in nature, but our synthetic world is full of them. The register of artificial substances lists over seven million.

Everyday solvents such as formaldehyde and alcohol, and other, more complex, substances, such as those used for dry cleaning, are also likely to end up in our fat—though often not in their original form. The real problem with these substances is their characteristic ability to precipitate liver damage with intensive short-term exposure or, in some cases, with long-term low-dose exposure, and it is this damage that the body seeks to avoid by dumping them in fat. So we have the additional possibility of some substances causing liver damage, thus helping other substances to gain access to our tissues.

At the core of the cause of each victim's PFR is the capacity of the liver to respond to the demands placed upon it by the avalanche of substances it has to deal with. If the liver is damaged or short of essential detoxifying agents, then the efficiency of the body's detoxification system may be greatly reduced. People whose livers are not functioning properly are bound to be more susceptible to the accumulation of toxic adiposity and the PFR Syndrome. This is because there is less capacity to detoxify than when the liver works at peak efficiency.

Such PFR victims include individuals who have suffered liver damage due to drugs, chemicals, or alcohol, as well as those who have had hepatitis (which means, literally, liver inflammation and has a variety of causes), malaria, Weil's disease, amebic dysentery, schistosomiasis, or allergic liver disease. And it will also include some of those who have difficulties in food absorption, or who are undernourished for any reason.

Many PFR sufferers will not realize that their livers are less efficient than normal. But some will know that they cannot tolerate more than a very small quantity of alcohol, or that they had a bad reaction to a hospital anesthetic, or that they have a tendency to get sick periodically, suffering nausea, indigestion, and headaches.

Clinical ecologists working in the field of allergic responses have identified what they term a subclinical illness. This is that vague feeling of being one or two degrees under, not up to much most of the time. This very widespread reaction is believed to be due to overload by low-level, environmental toxins. It may not be enough to trigger PFR in most people, but it should be taken as a warning of possible susceptibility.

While acute liver disease is fairly readily diagnosed by the jaundice that results, producing a yellow color in the skin as bile salts build up in the blood, the symptoms of chronic liver disease are vague. Sufferers feel generally sick, with indigestion, for the liver plays a crucial role in the digestion of food. In many cases, the liver does not come under suspicion for a long time—if at all.

There are chemical tests of liver function, but these are rather hit-and-miss; most can produce entirely normal results while disturbances in crucial enzyme systems go undetected. And even if the liver copes quite well much of the time, a slightly increased load on its detoxification capacity will mean that the protective system that produces fat deposition will come into play.

The whole question of the possible causes of PFR may seem impossibly grim. We don't want to diminish the size of the environmental problem that PFR represents, but once you understand how the body systems operate, you will see how you can work to overcome both cause and effects. It *is* possible to deal with them.

In Chapter 15 we explain liver function and the role of the liver in fat, food, and toxin metabolism in more detail. For now let us assure you that there is an answer to persistent fat retention. The people whose case histories were described are now happily back to normal and should remain at their ideal weight for the rest of their lives. You can do the same!

8

Are You What You Eat?

Most of us grew up with the assumption that we could eat anything, in any quantity, without coming to any real harm. We believed that if food or drink was on the supermarket shelf, it would be safe. It was only very recently that the dangers of relying on processed foods were recognized. The malnutrition in the midst of plenty, caused by junk foods, led to some questioning of the underlying assumption that if something was not actually dangerous, then it must be completely safe. Dieters discovered the problem of the empty calorie, enticing junk which caused nutritional problems.

Behind consumer awareness campaigns came the declaration that "you are what you eat," implying that if you relied on junk to feed and maintain you, you would turn into unhealthy junk. Many of us now accept the wisdom of avoiding junk food, although it is regrettably true that the profits of such businesses continue to grow.

The ideal that has always been pushed by dietitians and nutritionists is that of the balanced diet. What this usually amounts to is this: if your diet contains sufficient basic foods, with an emphasis on fresh fruit and vegetables, and is not short on protein, natural vitamins, and trace elements, you will be OK. Unfortunately, as the health statistics in general, and those for obesity specifically, show, either we have ignored this advice, or it is not completely correct.

Although many do ignore the basic common sense of such an approach to food, we believe that the ill health associated with food is out of all proportion to the imbalances in our national diet. The PFR Syndrome is part of this imbalance; many Life Profile cases had eating habits beyond reproach. We believe the possibility exists that a host of other specific conditions, as well as many minor illnesses, can be directly traced to what we are doing to our food.

While we have become aware of the health hazards of fast-food junk, we have been slow to react to other changes that have occurred over the past few decades. The whole food industry has been subjected to one of the most profound revolutions the world has ever experienced. But because of the strength of that assumption—if it's in the supermarket it must be OK—we have scarcely noticed what has been happening. We all know of the Green Revolution through statistics of the increase in crop yields, but the public-relations exercise fails to mention that these increases are bought at the cost of complete dependence upon expensive chemical input. The effects such crucial changes have had upon the nature of our foods has been hidden from us.

Other factors have helped to mask the profound changes that have taken place. One is the depopulation of the countryside; the majority of people are no longer involved in food production, whereas only a generation or so ago the reverse was true. We knew about the quality of food from direct personal experience; we were not fooled by the packaging as we are now. Another factor is our omnivorous nature; we can eat almost anything, and survive, if not thrive, on it. This capacity has colored our attitude to food, and it may have led us into complacent acceptance of things we should forcefully reject.

Our food has always been a source of potentially toxic substances. Indeed it was probably exposure to this risk throughout our evolution that led to the development of the liver's detoxifying capacity. By surviving the effects of poisonous plants and fruits, we learned to avoid them. Where sources of toxins were obvious, as with the leaves of potato or rhubarb, or the brightly colored berries of nightshade or laburnum, avoiding eating them was straightforward. But nature is not always so obvious. Many fungi contain poisons—not only the toadstools that cause confusion among the wild mushrooms, but also those microscopic varieties that make foods moldy. If you cannot see them, it may be difficult to avoid being poisoned.

Through the work of people like Louis Pasteur, this microsphere of life was uncovered and further defensive action taken. It is still true that invisible natural poisons kill many people in less developed parts of the world today; molds that grow on peanuts under warm, damp conditions of tropical regions cause thousands of deaths from liver cancer in those parts of the world. Some of these fungal poisons have been found to have uses; ergot, which grows on rye and used to cause a wide range of bizarre and fatal effects on those who ate a critical dose, now yields the antimigraine drug ergotamine. By and large, however, our ancestors would have found out by trial and error which foods were contaminated with invisible toxins. The capacity to survive mild poisoning was obviously an advantage; otherwise these lessons would have to be learned again by each generation.

Why is it so difficult to get wholesome food today? The simple answer is because of the food industry. Each part of the chain, from farmer to merchant, has forgotten what they are supposed to be doing—supplying the consumer with safe, wholesome produce. Farmers, who used to have a hard, healthy life in the great outdoors, are now heart-disease-prone agribusinessmen, extracting annual returns from sterile single-crop fields. And those storekeepers whose meat, fruit, and vegetables could once be judged by eye are now insulated by plastic wrap and corporate structures from the reality of their goods.

Today the invisible poisons we confront are no longer provided by nature; they are man-made. They are added to our food chains continually, from before birth or planting, throughout growth, during harvesting and storage, through all the subsequent processing, and right up to the time you eat the final product. In 1985 the cost of the chemicals used in food was almost $4 billion. Residues of pesticides can be found in most foods, even the fish caught in the open sea far from farm and factory. Processing additives are put into food for a variety of reasons and often consumers are persuaded to add their own dash of adulteration. All of these chemicals are, of course, considered "safe" by the relevant government institutions we assume are watching our interest in this area. But is this in fact the case? Mounting evidence points to an emphatic "No!"

We accept that each of the substances involved, in a low concentration, may be safe for the majority of people. And also that many people will be able to cope with a diet that contains many such substances. But we can only describe as very fortunate those who have bodies efficient enough to cope, day after day, with the assault that the modern food industry delivers.

The fact is that, as this assault grows in intensity and complexity, fewer and fewer people are able to cope. As our chemical loading grows with the progressive industrialization of food production, our protective systems are forced to work harder. Each new molecule has to be identified and decisions made about how it should be dealt with. The systems in our body that do this are finely tuned to deal with threats, which evolved relatively slowly in our biosphere, and they were very good at this. But asking them to cope with tens of thousands of totally artificial substances is like trying to use a flyswatter as a baseball bat; eventually breakdown is inevitable.

As food manufacturers seek to increase the shelf life and profitability of their products, more additives are used. It is these substances that cause the greatest problem for many people. In general terms, food that is high in additives is low in nutrition. Consuming such foods is a part of the degenerative cycle that can lead to PFR; your systems have to work harder to deal with them, for a lower reward. Of course, this fact has led to the suggestion that dieters could eat a lot of nonnutritional substances, thus feeling full without putting on weight. This is near the ultimate in using the body as a garbage can—treat it like one, and it will look like one. It will probably have exactly the opposite effect on your weight to the one you wanted.

You probably believe that, somewhere, someone is in control of the question of food-additive safety. In theory, food safety is monitored by the 1938 Federal Food, Drug, and Cosmetic Act. With all its numerous amendments, this act is probably the most extensive law of its kind in the world. The 1958 Delaney Clause amendment, which took effect in 1960, provided for the first time that no additive could be used in food unless the FDA (Food and Drug Administration), after a review of test data, considered it safe at intended levels of use. Additives in use at that time were designated GRAS, "generally recognized as safe." In 1980, the government began an extensive reevaluation of additives currently in use, and as a result the status of some additives has been changed. The Federal Food, Drug, and Cosmetic Act states that an acceptable additive must be safe, must not reduce the food's nutritional value or deceive the consumer, and must perform a useful function. Their widespread, uncontrolled use, however, makes a mockery of such complex regulations. Such exhortations are rather like asking a bank robber to observe the speed limit during his getaway.

Today there are somewhere around three thousand different food additives in use; no one is sure exactly how many. They are in such widespread use that on average a person consumes ten pounds of food additives each year (not counting sugar and salt). The food industry spent about $1 billion a year on additives.

There is also an endless array of both natural and synthetic food flavorings. Over two thousand flavorings are used by the food-processing industry; only about one quarter of these are natural. Precisely what many of these flavors are made of is considered a commercial secret. A raspberry flavoring for a food product that has to withstand high temperatures and pressures during manufacture may contain seven or more flavoring chemicals. The only people who know what these are work for the company that makes the product.

There is a growing wave of public concern about the whole question of additives, and many people think the government is dragging its feet. As we shall see, public concern may be justified if only on the grounds that the United States frequently allows substances that have been banned elsewhere, like BHA for instance, to go into our food.

As consumers we are generally led to believe that food additives would not be permitted if they had not been proved safe. But the present toxicity testing cannot be trusted to protect us

from the potential hazards of these chemicals. Dr. Eric Millstone of Sussex University, in England, reports that the direc-
tor of the British Industrial Biological Research Association
(BIBRA) has admitted that "food additive toxicology is . . .
merely a technology designed to produce animal test data sufficient to gain permission from governments for the use of additives." Further, it "is not a science which seeks to understand
the biological effects of chemicals upon humans."

As if this were not bad enough, the tests that are carried out
by toxicologists ignore the fact that we are exposed to a great
number of these substances at once. One particular food product may contain as many as thirty different additives, but they
are never tested in combination.

Nor can we rely on the animal tests that are carried out to
discover long-term effects on humans. The study of drug
effects has shown that reactions are frequently species-
specific. This means that a food additive that has no effect on
mice could be disastrous to humans, because although there
are many similarities, mice and men are different species. If
this additive causes serious damage to one person in a
thousand who consumes it, and minor damage to one in every
hundred, we might never know. Epidemiology, the counting of
the incidence of diseases among whole populations, would be
most unlikely to reveal the problem before it reached enormous
proportions. Think about cigarettes: they kill one in four of
lifetime smokers, yet for generations they were not identified
as dangerous.

The food-additive minefield is in many ways like prescription
drugs before thalidomide. Everyone assumes that things are
OK; everyone trusts the other person to behave reasonably; and
the momentum of the past keeps the system going. It is only
when some disaster occurs that any attention is paid to warnings. It is unlikely that food additives will produce a watershed
tragedy like thalidomide, yet there have been some deaths reported as the result of food additives. Furthermore, it must be
acknowledged that the load these substances place on the population as a whole is responsible for a slow-moving wave of
illness and fatigue, which inevitably grows with time. Slowly
developing phenomena always take time to be recognized. More

troubling is the fact that such large, slow waves take a long time to stop, even after their source and nature are recognized.

There are some other food additives already known to produce illness in a disturbingly large proportion of people. The best documented example is tartrazine (FD&C Yellow No. 5), a yellow coloring. Professor Maurice Hanssen described tartrazine as "a very commonly used color." It can cause skin rashes, hayfever (ironically, it was used to color antihistamine tablets), breathing problems, blurred vision, gastric upsets, and purple blotches on the skin. Just how many people are susceptible to these effects is a matter of wide controversy. It has been estimated that a hundred thousand Americans are sensitive to tartrazine.

Naturally, the food industry argues that such risks are minimal. And they are supported by the Allergic Diseases Section of the Laboratory of Clinical Investigation of the National Institutes of Health (NIH) and the Asthma and Allergy Foundation. Both these groups feel that food allergy is relatively rare, affecting no more than 5 to 10 percent of the population. Dr. Dean D. Metcalfe of NIH has stated that clearly 20 to 30 percent of people who seek treatment for food allergy are suffering from something else. Because many allergic symptoms are nonspecific—vague abdominal discomfort, tension, fatigue, headaches, depression, and trouble concentrating—they are hard to diagnose and are frequently dismissed by physicians as exaggerated. Meanwhile thousands go on suffering discomfort while being additionally plagued by weight they cannot lose. Both of these problems may stem from eating substances that are toxic.

Tartrazine is one of a group of FD&C certified food colors which are derived from coal tar. All have been implicated in hyperactivity, and some, such as FD&C Red No. 2—amaranth—have been linked with tumors in animals. Amaranth has been banned in the United States since 1976.

Some of the most dangerous of the additives used in the U.S. are the butylated antioxidants, BHA and BHT. They are added to fats to prevent rancidity and may be found in margarine, vegetable oils, and many baked products containing fat. They have been linked with allergic reactions and kidney and liver problems. The FDA has BHT on a list of additives that require further study. Yet BHT is found in almost every processed food containing fat or oil, as well as chewing gum, candy, and dry breakfast cereals.

The benzoates (benzoic acid and sodium benzoate) are preservatives and mold retardants. Benzoyl peroxide is used to bleach flour. These chemicals are known to be hazardous to allergy sufferers and have been restricted in the USSR, because they cause brain damage and convulsions, and retard growth in animals.

The nitrates (sodium nitrate and sodium nitrite) are also used as preservatives. It is these additives that give the pink color to meat products. Nitrates are broken down to nitrites in the body and, to some degree, during cooking. They interact with amines from food and drugs to produce nitrosamines, which are carcinogenic. These additives can also cause allergic reactions, are implicated in arthritis, and may interfere with the ability of the liver to store vitamin A. They have been banned in Norway.

Sulfites (sulfur dioxide, potassium metabisulfite, sodium sulfite, sodium metabisulfite, sodium bisulfite, potassium bisulfite) are preservatives, antioxidants, and bleaches. They are to be found in the highest concentrations in dried fruit—especially apricots and other bright-colored fruit, for they stop them from turning brown. They are also used in wines, beer, fruit juices and purees, soft drinks, jam, and dried vegetables, and in salad bars. They destroy vitamin E and the B vitamins and may cause genetic mutations. Some people are allergic to them, particularly asthmatics. Since 1982, there have been 1,400 complaints of reactions to sulfites and reports that at least 13 people have died as the result of sulfitic agents. Sulfites are also added to more than 1,100 drugs to protect their potency. In spite of their widespread use and reports of serious reactions to them, action to limit or ban the use of sulfites has been slow. In short, it seems that other federal agencies that regulate sulfites are waiting to see what the FDA will do, while the FDA is in no hurry to act.

Glutamates (monosodium glutamate, glutamic acid) are "flavor enhancers." The most used and the best known is monosodium glutamate (MSG). This was found to be the cause of "Chinese restaurant syndrome," a reaction typified by headaches, nausea, dizziness, and pains in the neck, which can occur after a meal heavy in MSG.

A list of food additives, with information on which to avoid and which are believed to be safe, appears in Appendix 1. They are not all potentially hazardous; in fact, some are valuable components of our normal diet. For example, carotene, which is transformed into vitamin A in our bodies, is a natural yellow dye with no known adverse effects. It is often added to margarine and cakes.

The moves toward improved food labeling are intended to help people who are worried about additives to identify those foods that may cause them problems. While this is helpful, additives are only part of the problem. They are the most obvious form of chemical contamination of our food, but they may not be the most dangerous. Pesticide residues in food are both more poisonous and harder to identify.

For farmworkers, spraying land with noxious chemicals has become a common job. Increases in cancer deaths and birth defects among their children reveal the effects of this change among this previously very healthy group of workers. The furrows left in fields by the spraying machinery are everywhere. During spring and early summer farming areas should, in our opinion, be closed to the public as health hazards.

The Environmental Protection Agency controls pesticide use, setting tolerance levels. In spite of the highly toxic nature of the many substances involved, very few of the pesticides that the EPA has allowed have been thoroughly and rigorously tested. Although maximum residue levels are fixed by the EPA, it is not always easy to detect produce with residues that exceed these limits. Laurie Mott, project scientist at the Natural Resource Defense Council, has said, "The pesticide industry has undue influence on the decision making process. . . ."

Jay Feldman of the National Coalition Against the Misuse of Pesticides said the EPA is moving too slowly, reflecting a White House decision on priorities. "There is a trade-off between defense and health and the environment," he said. "We have a national emergency in this country when it comes to our drinking water and food supply. There are 50,000 pesticide formulations in our environment and we know very little about them."

Pesticides must be used with discretion because they are designed to kill some living organism. Many pesticides are so highly toxic that very small quantities can kill a person, and exposure to a sufficient amount of almost any pesticide can make a person sick. Even fairly safe pesticides can irritate the skin, eyes, nose, or mouth.

Against this background, the rate of spraying increases yearly as farmers get more and more dependent on pesticides. A dangerous new cycle has been set up. It started with the excessive use of artificial fertilizers; these gave improved crop yields, which encouraged farmers to break away from the traditional mixture of crop rotation and alternating land use for crops and for grazing, which maintained a continuing, natural soil fertility. Having broken this tradition, farmers had little choice other than to fertilize; this reduced the natural resilience of both soil and crops, so they had to use pesticides to limit pests. These still further reduce the soil's resilience, so more pesticides have to be used. . . . Today farming is little better than an extractive industry, drawing contaminated crops from dead soil.

There are six hundred active ingredients in the fifty thousand pesticides available. One-half to two-thirds of these are authorized for use on food crops. Only ninety of these pesticides have been registered. This does not mean that even these few are safe, only that the EPA has determined what additional tests are needed. Eighty-five percent of the land where citrus fruits, apples, and potatoes are grown has been treated with insecticides. More than 50 percent of corn, peanut, and potato farmland is treated with herbicides. More than 70 percent of apple and citrus crops are treated with fungicides. Residues on raw products, such as fresh apples, are not subject to the FDA Delaney Clause regulating cancer-causing substances.

Farmers spray more and more just to maintain a constant level of crop "quality." The reasons for this are well recognized, and the result is described as the "pesticide treadmill." In addition to the decrease in natural soil fertility, intensive, mechanized agriculture leads to increasing use of pesticides, because the natural resistance of crops to pests is decreasing while the pests' resistance to chemicals is increasing. At the same time, spraying kills the normal predators of pests, so that the biological controls that used to operate become ineffective.

In the past, pest levels were kept down by crop rotation, plowing, and a natural balance between species; varieties of crops were selected for their ability to resist pests, and the quality of the soil was kept high enough to allow them to grow strong so that pests did not attack them too readily. And if lettuces arrived at the stores with aphids (small green insects) on them, cabbages with the odd caterpillar, apples with occasional worms, nobody worried too much—it was only natural, after all.

If there are no controls down on the farm, what about controls on the produce that we eat? The Environmental Protection Agency regulates the Federal Insecticide, Fungicide, and Rodenticide Act, which is supposed to control pesticide residues in food. To this end, it states that food must be fit for human consumption and not injurious to health. The FDA enforces the EPA regulations to control pesticide levels on food. However, the tests commonly used can detect only 107 of the 268 pesticides that have tolerance levels permanently established by the FDA. Twenty pesticides suspected of causing cancer are known to be in the food supply and not monitored by the FDA.

The FDA also investigates instances of food poisoning. While salmonella and similar bacterial problems can present a health hazard, the risk is relatively small among healthy populations. The government, its legislation, and the practices of those carrying out policy just have not kept up-to-date with the changing reality of the modern world. The function of the FDA's parent organization, the U.S. Department of Agriculture (USDA), is to encourage the agricultural production of food. It retreats into a secretive shell when confronted with the possibility that drenching all our food with lethal poisons may be hazardous to health.

Food additives and pesticides may be in a pre-thalidomide situation. The best analogy is that of the situation, beloved in Victorian melodrama, where the most poisonous substances, like arsenic, could be bought over the counter at the local drug-gist, no questions asked. Later, villains could be caught by examination of the "poisons book"—if they were not clever enough to forge a signature. As we shall see, even the control of substances acknowledged to be dangerous and supposedly banned is roughly in a pre-"poisons book" stage.

The political reality of the pesticide situation also works against our search for pure food. The government's encourage-ment of agribusiness is aided and abetted by the chemical com-panies, most of them powerful multinationals, and reinforced by the farmers' lobby, one of the most powerful pressure groups in the country. So change will be slow. Nevertheless, the scale of the problem is beginning to be realized.

A recent study of California-grown produce published by the Natural Resources Defense Council (NRDC), in which the in-vestigators collected a total of 71 samples of 12 vegetables and fruits (broccoli, carrots, cucumbers, eggplants, grapes, lettuces, oranges, peppers, potatoes, spinach, strawberries, and zuc-chini), showed residues of DDT, DDE, kelthane, trifluralin, methidathione, chlorporphan, dieldrin, endosulfan, Dacthal, dicloran, malathion, mevinphos, endrin, aldicarb, diazionon and parathion. Nearly half of the samples contained residues of at least one of 19 pesticides, and 42 percent contained residues of more than one chemical. A few samples had traces of up to four. The only conclusion to be drawn is that nothing was def-initely safe.

You may think that analyzing only this small sample in Cal-ifornia is not enough to cause general alarm about all U.S. produce. That is wrong! California supplies the country with 51 percent of its fresh market produce each year. This is a telling sample of the enormous problem that exists. Although the Environmental Protection Agency sets allowable levels of pesticides, it does not enforce these limits.

The Food and Drug Administration takes care of enforce-ment. With current budget cutbacks, inspectors in the near future may be working shorter hours, leaving the possibility open for a weaker inspection system. Coupled with this is the fact that the equipment used by the FDA personnel to measure residues can detect traces of only about one-third of the pesticides registered for use on food. Often the laboratory results of FDA spot checks on produce aren't available until after the food has been sold. Yet the government keeps assuring us that this system is a safeguard!

Even more worrisome than the laughable testing methods of the FDA is the type of residue found by the analysts. Some residues were the particularly persistent and dangerous kinds that are not approved for use on food anymore, such as DDT (banned in 1972) and its breakdown product DDE, as well as dieldrin (banned in 1974) and endrin (banned in 1979).

A recent review of over six hundred published studies found that in the U.S., people with no occupational exposure have measurable residues of 94 chemical contaminants in their bodies; of these, 20 are pesticides and their breakdown products. Besides the harm to humans, pesticide use causes many unplanned and undesirable environmental effects: beneficial species (like songbirds) are killed; spray drifting away from the treated area contaminates nearby areas; wildlife dies, along with honeybees and other pollinating insects—not to mention the pollution of air, water, soil, and other plants.

DDT was the insecticide that gave rise to the situation described in Rachel Carson's classic book, *Silent Spring*. DDT is banned or severely restricted in many countries around the world. This widespread condemnation is based on the serious health risks to both humans and wildlife—DDT is responsible for the virtual extinction of herons, falcons, hawks, eagles, and other birds of prey in the U.S. and elsewhere. It accumulates in fat and causes liver damage. DDT keeps turning up, because it is a very persistent chemical with a half-life of as long as twenty years. Young mothers are aware of the legacy of DDT as their breast milk is contaminated with it.

After the scare caused in the early 1960s by the realization of the hazards, it was generally assumed that the problem had been solved. However, this is not the case. The herbicide dioxin, one of the most poisonous substances known, has been widely used on fruit trees, rice crops, and cattle rangeland. It is also used as a wood preservative in barns and animal feed bins. Recent tests have shown that fish and beef contain dioxin in the range of 3 to 40 parts per trillion. Overexposure to dioxin causes chloracne (a severe form of acne), decreased liver function, cirrhosis of the liver, stomach ulcers, nervous system damage, and mental disturbances, such as memory lapses and depression. A recent report noted that a baby who is breast-fed for one year gets eighteen times its lifelong limit of dioxin. This exposure results from the fact that the mother's fat stores are used to make breast milk. These fat stores have accumulated high levels of dioxin and other fat-soluble toxins during the mother's lifetime.

Other chlorinated hydrocarbons, PCBs (polychlorinated biphenyls), used in the manufacture of heavy electrical equipment, still contaminate our food supply even though their use was banned in 1976. For many years prior to this, PCBs were routinely dumped into major waterways such as the Hudson River. Striped bass that spend a lot of time in the Hudson River have contamination levels above the safe limit set by the Food and Drug Administration. Because of this, fishing for striped bass in New York waters was banned in 1986. Before 1986, the Department of Environmental Conservation had been advising children and pregnant women not to eat any striped bass and others not to eat it more than once a week.

Current laboratory techniques are not sensitive enough to measure the tiny amounts of pesticide residues that may be able to cause illness. In the summer of 1985, there were 1,175 cases of poisoning, resulting in six deaths and two stillbirths, that were linked to eating contaminated California watermelons. Temik (aldicarb sulfoxide), a highly toxic pesticide, commonly used on potatoes and cirtrus fruits, was responsible for the outbreak, which was the largest pesticide-related poisoning incident ever reported in the U.S.

Although laboratory testing of the melons showed no traces of Temik, the outbreak was brought under control after all the watermelons in California's food-distribution system were destroyed. California has ordered farmers not to use Temik on watermelons, and the Environmental Protection Agency is reviewing registration of the chemical. A report issued by the Centers for Disease Control stated, "It is possible that the laboratory analyses are too insensitive to detect [the poison] at levels that can cause human illness."

Alar (daminozide), a pesticide suspected of being a carcinogen, is the most commonly used growth regulator in the apple-growing industry. Over 610,000 pounds of the pesticide is used yearly to grow larger, redder, and firmer apples with a long shelf life. When exposed to heat or acid, as when raw apples are cooked into applesauce or pie filling, a more dangerous cancer-causing by-product, UDMH (unsymmetrical dimethylhydrozine), is formed. Alar residues have been found in apple juice and other apple products in the supermarket.

The EPA refused to ban Alar, stating that studies had not been "completely definitive." A ban will be considered again in 1988 when further testing by Uniroyal, the manufacturer of Alar, is completed. In the meantime, the EPA has established regulations for its use. The EPA's action has been criticized by consumer and environmental groups, who support the ban on Alar and consider that the EPA has failed to protect the public, particularly infants and children, from pesticide residues.

So far we have discussed processed foods, and fruit and vegetables. The situation with meat products is, if anything, even more hazardous. There is growing resistance among consumers to the factory farming of animals. In spite of this, 99 percent of the meat we eat is produced in this way.

Factory farming is so unnatural that it only works when the animals are continually drugged. This is done both to control diseases, which are endemic under such conditions, and to stimulate growth. The latter involves hormones and antibiotics, administered in food, by injection, or implantation. To further complicate this problem, the waste products of some animals are fed to others—for example, the waste from factory-farmed chickens is fed to intensively reared pigs.

A congressional report, "Human Food Safety and the Regulation of Animal Drugs," prepared early in 1986, charges that the Food and Drug Administration inadequately monitors the use of toxic drugs and nutrition supplements in raising livestock. Thousands of drugs and supplements used by farmers to make animals grow faster and stay healthy have never been approved for use by the FDA and so are being "marketed in violation of federal law." Many drugs that have been identified as carcinogenic are still in use. In 1977, methylene blue, a drug suspected of causing cancer and genetic damage, was used to neutralize nitrate poisoning in cattle. The FDA allowed it to be sold, even though it had never received formal approval. In addition, sales and use of unregulated animal drugs imported from Eastern Europe and Asia have not been controlled. Only 7 percent of the thousands of animal drugs on the market have been identified and inventoried by the FDA, in spite of the fact that this is in direct violation of a statute that requires the agency to maintain an inventory of all approved animal drugs.

Monitoring drug residues in beef, poultry, pork, and milk is another function of the FDA that has been criticized. The agency's scientists have not developed the chemical-analysis techniques necessary to detect many toxic residues.

Animals treat these substances in exactly the same way that we do: they metabolize many of them into their flesh. In addition to the development of resistant strains of bacteria, such as salmonella, from the liberal use of antibiotics, which pose a direct risk to humans, the metabolized products of the chemical assault these animals have to withstand are passed on to us.

In 1984, there were eighteen cases of food poisoning, including one death, linked to eating hamburgers infected with a strain of salmonella bacteria that was resistant to antibiotics. The Centers for Disease Control state that the use of antibiotics to increase the weight of cattle and prevent disease was to blame for the outbreak.

Official controls on these poisons in our food are, in practical terms, nonexistent. Government action amounts, at best, to lip service to consumer protection, at worst to deception. In reality, their priority is the protection of the interests of farmers and chemical companies, not those of ordinary consumers.

The growing risk of residue contamination is a major regulatory problem for the Food Safety and Inspection Service (FSIS). The agency was forced to cut the number of inspectors by 521 persons in 1986 and to eliminate over 400 part-time and temporary positions.

Many of the substances we have been discussing are powerful biocides. Their purpose is to kill living things. While they may not kill you, they will kill some part of you. It is in fighting a desperate battle to protect you that your body is driven to maintain those fat stores. The only way you can safely escape from PFR is to stop this battle. Stop loading your system with food that should be classed as unfit for human consumption.

Take the battle outside your body. Just as you should not treat it as a garbage can, neither should you allow it to be a battlefield. You are what you eat. If you eat poisoned or contaminated food, you will be poisoned and contaminated. If your body cannot cope with this, it will react adversely. One of the ways it can react is by making you fat.

9

Escape PFR—The Plan

Having read this far, you will have a pretty good idea of the situation you are in. You know that persistent fat is the product of a unique interaction between your metabolism and the many substances you are exposed to in your food and your environment. Escaping PFR probably seems to be an overwhelming prospect. Being stuck with weight you do not want, caused by factors that may appear to be largely beyond your control, can seem like being caught in a trap. But do not despair—escape is possible!

What you need is a good plan and a cool head. We can provide the plan; you have to provide the personal qualities. Like all successful escape plans, it depends upon coordination, timing, and the ability to understand what is happening to you as you work your way through. We warned that this book was for those who seriously wanted to lose that excess weight. This is where we start to get serious.

We would like you to read this and the following three chapters before you attempt to take any action. When you have done this, you will understand what is involved in The Plan. This is important because The Plan provides an integrated strategy; each part must be used in order, and in the correct relationship with the other parts. You may find it helpful to make notes of things that particularly apply to you and your situation as you read. There are also some initial steps you can take to get you ready to apply The Plan, and these are noted in this chapter.

We must once more stress the importance of individual differences. Because no two people are identical and we all live different lives, no single answer will produce the same effect on all of us. An important part of the success of The Plan is this: as you work through it, you will be learning about yourself. You must use this knowledge to judge the emphasis you need to give to each part of The Plan—how important diet is to you, how much contamination you can tolerate, how fast your progress should be. In short, you must be in control.

You are the active ingredient in The Plan. Being a passive accepter of other people's diets, food products, and environmental pollution has contributed to your PFR Syndrome. Now you must be assertive; you must start to fight back, and we'll point you in the right direction. The ultimate objective is to learn to live in a way that suits your system and capacities best.

You will need high motivation; we will take that for granted. And you will need a fair measure of faith. Not in us, or this book, but in yourself. You must learn to trust the signals from your body, to be able to look at yourself realistically, and to interpret any ambiguous signals accurately. When you understand what is happening to you, and why, then you will be in control.

Before getting down to details of The Plan, we must deal with the most likely cause of possible failure to solve your PFR problem. You will fail if you do not care about yourself enough. You have to psych yourself up in the same way that performers and athletes do before a big event, because you have a lot of barriers to break through in your escape. The reason that PFR is so common is that it is a reflection of values in our society. You have to care enough and be strong enough to start going against the grain. You are fighting for yourself. At first you may feel lonely and overwhelmed. Don't—there are many more like you out there in the same battle; you will make friends and allies!

You will say, of course, that the reason you want to lose weight and be thin and fit is precisely because you do care about yourself. Our experience indicates, however, that a lot of people go in for dieting, and even exercise, because they do not care. They are using dieting as a way of punishing or rejecting their essential selves. Both the issues of female sexuality and the addition of body fat, in the context of a generally repressive social background, create such a minefield for developing young women that fat and guilt become closely associated. Punishing the metabolism is the modern form of mortification of the flesh.

As your first preparatory step, try looking at yourself naked in a full-length mirror. Turn round, check yourself out all over, and write down your feelings about what you see. What are your best features, and what could do with some improvement? Your answers may indicate that you have to escape from some psychological traps before you can successfully tackle your PFR problem.

Our culture teaches women self-rejection, almost self-abasement. We want you to look at yourself and feel pride, justifiable pride, in what you are and what you can become. Reject shallow narcissism that tells you to paint it over or cover it up with fabric. Modesty, false or real, is a route to submission and rejection. Look at the real you frequently and with growing, honest pride in the wonder of your body and yourself. You and those around you will be much better for your changed attitude.

The way you look at yourself may also indicate other bits of psychological baggage that you just do not need. Do you have unrealistic expectations about yourself? Losing weight will not make you taller or shorter. Although your bone structure will change, this takes a long time and does not significanuy affect height or proportions. Be realistic about the importance of weight loss in your life. We have one Life Profile client who is keeping her fat because she uses it to make her husband feel sorry for her, and thus maintains the "helpless woman" role that is apparently important to their relationship. This is an extreme case, but had she been able to be honest at the start she would have saved herself a lot of halfhearted effort.

This book is not about the psychological aspects of weight problems, but the importance of these aspects should not be overlooked. If you have any doubts at all in this area that may upset your motivation to escape PFR, check them out. You could follow up with one of the books on the psychology of self-acceptance. We recommend Suzie Orbach's excellent *Fat Is a Feminist Issue.*

So before you start, it is important to be sure of yourself and your motivation!

The escape plan was designed primarily to deal with the PFR Syndrome, and it is not a weight-loss diet in the normal sense. Conventional approaches do not work for people with TAT, because as the old joke has it, "you can't get there from here."

To deal with PFR, you have to gear your systems up to higher levels of health and give your metabolism greater capacity. That is the way you can get there. Of course, The Plan will make you thinner—that is its primary objective—but not without making you a lot healthier in the process.

You have taken the first preparatory step by looking at yourself. Now take the second: affirm your own unique value. Write in your notebook, "I am the most important thing in my life." Write it until you believe it and can act on that belief without a second thought.

An important part of your new self-appreciation is to understand this: if you are a PFR victim, have TAT you would rather be without, then your body has been doing an excellent job in protecting you from pollutants in your environment. Acknowledge that, look on that fat with new and wiser eyes, perhaps even appreciate what those extra pounds may have saved you from. Now make up your mind that you will return the favor and protect your body. Start by deciding "I am not a garbage dump, and my body is not going to be treated like one."

The Plan has three separate aspects, each forming a distinct stage, which interact to produce their effect. The stages must be initiated one after another. When the results of each progressive stage are added together, their effects build up and complement each other. We will outline them in the order you need to carry them out.

1. *Detoxification.* Until the level of whatever substances your system is treating as toxic is drastically reduced in your blood-

stream and liver, your body will not be ready to allow its fat stores to shrink.

2. *Increasing Metabolic Capacity.* This means creating the conditions in which your liver can rebuild itself and begin to handle greater quantities of toxins. Fortunately this process will start automatically as the stress imposed on it is reduced. The Plan is designed both to assist this process and to increase your liver's capacity to deal with loads it may encounter in the future.

3. *Mobilizing Fat.* This is the final and crucial stage. It cannot be achieved until your liver has sufficient capacity to cope with the toxins stored in this tissue.

To ensure that this capacity is at its highest, the life-style changes initiated in the first two stages must be firmly established and maintained throughout the third.

Warning: Losing toxic adipose tissue in any other way can cause serious illness. You will be releasing poisons from their storage in your fat; this must be done with extreme care and sensitivity to what is happening. Do not try to short-circuit The Plan.

Now that you have the outline of The Plan, are you ready to take the third preliminary step? If you have bathroom scales, throw them away. (You could give them to a man, for whom they are more relevant, or donate them to charity.) Remember, we are concerned with the *quality* of your flesh, not its *quantity*. Just as your body should not be treated as a garbage dump, neither should it be thought of as a sack of potatoes. Go back to your mirror, learn to look at yourself, see what you are, recite "I am the most important thing in my life," and determine to work toward what you want to be.

While carrying out the first two stages of The Plan, detoxification and increasing metabolic capacity, you may not lose any weight at all. On the other hand you might be one of the lucky ones for whom detoxification, or increasing metabolic capacity, is enough in itself to solve the problem. You may even put on a little more weight. Do not panic—this is where you need that cool head! Understand what is going on and carry on with The Plan.

Whichever way your metabolism reacts, you will start to feel better and more energetic with every week you stay on The Plan. When you do come up to the third stage of The Plan, you will find it poses few problems for you—providing you have got the first two stages right.

It is essential that you do not try to go straight to part three. You will not escape. The only route out of PFR is to take care of your toxic intake, then improve the state of your liver. Any other way will just take you back to square one, on the diet/fat seesaw, with more fat than you started with. Then you will have to go back to the beginning and start again, because you will have overlooked the fundamental cause of your weight gain. Do it once, and do it right!

If you become sick at any point while working on The Plan, you may have to drop back a stage. Illness puts a demand on the liver; it has to deal with bacteria and the debris produced when the immune system fights off infections. Put yourself in a holding pattern until the condition has cleared up.

And if you must take medicines, remember they will be putting an additional direct load on your detoxifying systems. Bear in mind that roughly 90 percent of medication is not a matter of life or death; it is given not to cure, but to suppress symptoms. If you are in any doubt, check this with your physician, and remember that there are almost always alternative options. Drugs are essential only when there is no alternative and they are fulfilling some function beyond symptomatic relief. Almost all over-the-counter medicines only suppress symptoms, and you can manage without them. The sensible thing to do, if you are on medication, is first to discuss the real need with your doctor, and while continuing with the therapy if it is essential, seek an alternative solution that has less toxic potential.

Illness, when you are working on the final stage of The Plan, *mobilizing fat,* may be an indication that you are pushing yourself too hard. Illness could be your body's way of protesting. Try easing off a little; make progress more slowly. And make absolutely sure you are maintaining the changes initiated in the first stages of The Plan.

Finally, mobilizing fat and coping with illness are both hard work; make sure you are getting enough good, wholesome food to eat, particularly fresh fruit and vegetables. Remember the aim is to work with your body and its systems, not against them.

STAGE ONE: DETOXIFICATION

Detoxification is a gentle process. It means removal from your system and environment of those substances that your metabolism has chosen to treat as toxic. Every individual will react differently to a wide range of potentially toxic substances; you will need to identify those that are causing a problem for you so that you can avoid contact with them. Detailed advice and help with this task is given in Chapter 11.

As we have seen, the most important single route for toxic substances into your system is through eating and drinking. Everything we put in our mouths is assessed by our immune systems. If they decide it is safe, no action is taken. If they make a mistake, classing as unsafe something which is actually safe, you may suffer an allergic response. If they decide it is toxic, a whole range of defensive mechanisms may swing into action. We are mainly concerned with substances that pass through this net as safe, but are later reclassified because they cause an overload.

You will have realized from previous chapters that almost everything you swallow goes through the warehouse of the liver for processing. It is here that the crucial overload occurs, and where we must reduce the stress. To do this you will have to be very careful about the substances that you expect your system to process.

The key to success is to realize that things are not always what they seem. If you were asked to judge which was most toxic, a glass of red wine or a glass of whiskey, the answer might seem simple. Whiskey has more alcohol, and is therefore more toxic to your system—true—but what if you are sensitive to the sterilizers, inhibitors, colorings, or other things that tend to get into some red wines but will not be found in a good whiskey?

This is why our dietary advice is based on the idea of innocent food. You should only eat or drink things that have been subject to minimal processing, ideally none at all. Your food should be, as far as is possible, innocent of any contamination.

We will give specific advice on this later. For now, let us deal with common background problems. Survey after survey has revealed that shoppers judge how fresh and wholesome food is by the packaging. Now, while we are sure you are not dumb enough to be taken in by plastic wrap, bright lights, and a slick label, bear in mind that a lot of people are. If they were not, the whole food-packaging industry would disappear. Its main concern is to get products into standard packs, that fit in standard boxes, that load on standard dollies, that fit in standard trucks. It is little wonder that everything possible is done to standardize the food at the beginning of this process. Nature is far from perfect. Ignore the packaging. Look at what you are going to eat, not what you are going to throw away.

When did you last see an honest vegetable advertised on TV? As a rough, general rule, if they have to advertise processed food on TV, you should not buy it. To make them profitable, such products have to have an entire range of industrial processing, standardizing, preserving, packaging, warehousing, and delivery behind them. Such food is made the way Henry Ford made cars, and you are the scrap heap at the end of the line. Worse, you are expected to pay for the privilege of taking in all the junk!

If you are one of the growing number of people who have food allergies, the basic contamination of your food may be at the heart of your problem. If you are wrestling with an elimination diet, try our recommendations. It may not be the food after all, and your elimination diet could be depriving you of important nutrients. If, however, you confirm that it is the food you are reacting against, then you will have to adapt the dietary rules we give to apply to your particular case. We firmly believe that the foundation of many allergic reactions, from food allergies to hayfever, is the pollution we subject ourselves to. The PFR diet and detoxification strategies will assist with these conditions.

You must also be wary of foods advertised as pure, whole, wholesome, "with nothing taken out." None of this means nothing has been put in. An increasing number of growers and manufacturers are realizing that there is a growing market for good wholesome food and drink. Some use every opportunity to bend descriptions as far as they can without breaking the law. Your best guide is to read the labels carefully; your best action is to follow the dietary rules we give in Chapter 10.

For most people it remains true that the most potent toxins they are likely to encounter on a day-to-day basis are alcohol, cigarette smoke, and prescribed drugs. Remembering the wine/whiskey question, you will have to judge the contribution alcohol and cigarettes might be making to your problem; the only safe advice we can give is that you avoid them completely until you have solved your PFR problem. Appendix 2 lists commonly prescribed drugs that are acknowledged to cause weight gain in some individuals. However, this list is bound to be incomplete because weight gain may be a side effect of a particular drug for only a few individuals. The effect may not have been recognized or researched with other drugs, or it may be an individual response.

Drugs are a difficult problem. We are conditioned to believe that they are an unquestionable good and that there is no alternative to their use. If you have to take medication, you may not be able to avoid stressing your liver, and, in the absence of any viable alternative, you may have to accept that dealing with PFR will be that much more difficult for you.

Processed food additives will put a load on your liver. In the U.S., the average person now eats a staggering ten pounds of these chemicals every year. Just look at ten pounds of flour next time you are in a supermarket! And as this is an average and many people in the know avoid them, try to imagine how much some people must consume. Our description of bodies as garbage dumps is not an exaggeration. We will explain how to cut down on this load, and Appendix 1 has a guide to the hazards of some additives.

In addition to the substances added to processed food, we have to avoid the residues of chemicals and drugs used to treat it during growth and storage. The quantity of pesticide residues we consume can't be measured. Amounts will vary from one food to another and among different crops of the same food. Once more, the only safe thing is to avoid chemical- and drug-treated foods as much as possible. More details of this aspect of the PFR problem are given in Chapter 10.

The last source of potential toxins we have to deal with is the immediate environment, particularly the air you breathe. We can all control the pollution we release into the air in our homes, and this is the best place to start. You may be naive enough to believe that there is no pollution in your home—if only that were true!

All those "cleansers," polishes, and sprays, and even the "air fresheners," are nothing short of chemical pollution on the domestic level. Remember the rule about TV advertising, and think what it is that actually makes things shiny, germ-free, "more fresh, more flowery, smelling more natural than ever before." That's right, artificial molecules produced by the chemical industry. Their main effects are to fool our senses and confuse our detoxification systems. But you do not have to go along with it. Advice on detoxifying the home without being overrun by germs is given in Chapter 11.

If your major problem turns out to be with fumes at work, you may have to consider changing your job. We know this is not easy, but there may really be little choice. How much are you willing to suffer and risk for the job and the money it brings? You may be able to exert pressure to get working conditions improved, but it isn't always easy to do. It takes a lot of dead or deformed victims before industry changes its methods.

STAGE TWO: INCREASING METABOLIC CAPACITY

Increasing metabolic capacity is not as complicated in practice as it is in theory. You will already have gained some capacity by detoxifying yourself and your immediate environment. The next stage, which has two phases—*recovery* and *warming up*—will build on this good work.

If you have been exposed to anything that has damaged your liver, such as a lot of alcohol, you may have a fairly long job on your hands. Fortunately those highly active and complex liver cells are capable of regeneration under appropriate conditions.

Even if you have killed some off, it will be possible to compensate for the losses.

It is crucial to the success of The Plan that you maintain your detoxified diet and environment while you are increasing your metabolic capacity. It is equally important that you do not try to burn any of your TAT off until you have as much metabolic capacity working for you as you can possibly muster. If you don't have the capacity to cope with the toxins in the adipose tissue, your system will just short-circuit, dumping them straight back into fat.

The lengths to which you may have to go to achieve this capacity may seem extreme, but remember you are escaping from a desperate situation. The PFR Syndrome is common among women because their livers are more limited in capacity than are those of men. So one obvious part of the answer is to reduce this imbalance as much as possible. That is the focus of the third stage.

STAGE THREE: MOBILIZING FAT

To mobilize fat, it may be necessary to convince your system that you are more masculine than you actually are. By behaving in ways that are subtly more masculine, specifically in the way you use physical energy, you will encourage your hormones and liver to respond accordingly. What you will, in effect, be doing is encouraging your liver to act more like the male liver. The larger male liver provides men with explosive energy because the liver cells store glycogen, which is released by adrenaline to fuel activity. In this way the liver acts as a glycogen energy battery; the same process happens in the female liver, but to a lesser degree. The objective is to increase the capacity of this particular function. Of course, this cannot occur without the liver building up its other capacities—which is the effect we are after.

This process will not really make you more masculine. Just as your system has been misled by the chemicals that have caused your PFR problem, so your solution may be to mislead it a little the other way. You will not get masculine muscles (unless you want them!), nor will you notice any other changes toward maleness.

The principles involved in The Plan are those which maximize health and healing, and they inevitably spill over into improved athletic ability. So even if the idea is a little strange, the effect will be completely beneficial. Those who are very overweight may have to spend a little more time and effort increasing their metabolic capacity before finally escaping, but don't worry, you will make it.

Mobilizing fat needs patience. With PFR, your body will not readily let you take off the fat you want to lose. Passive dieting will not work; even starvation will not shift it. You will have to burn it off in a controlled manner. In doing this, you will use your enhanced metabolic capacity. And that "hangover" effect mentioned earlier will serve as a warning if you attempt to go too fast! It will tell you that you are releasing too much toxic material into your system. You will have to start off slowly, but the more weight you lose, the faster it will come off.

The only way to mobilize this fat is to burn it up by working your body; this is why we call this phase *revving up*. This is where your active commitment to losing weight will really be tested. Using your body, being physically active, not only makes you physically competent, but also further enhances the competence of your metabolism. It is in this final phase that you will break through, both to being thin and to gaining that additional fitness and health that will keep you thin.

Even if you hate the idea, don't despair. Your dislike of being physically active could be part of a vicious and self-sustaining circle. If you are very overweight, using your body may seem unpleasant, so you will tend to become more overweight. Inside you is a vibrant, physical animal, capable of pleasure and joy in activity. Let yourself go. It is part of your escape from PFR.

After you have solved your PFR problem, you can go on to create the kind of body you have always desired. In Chapter 14, we will explain the principles behind body contouring, and how you can keep the kind of shape you want for the rest of your life.

That is the outline of the escape plan, and we are sure you will agree that it is different. But then so is the problem it is designed to deal with. In the rest of this chapter we will try to anticipate questions that may have come into your mind.

No, The Plan does not involve dieting. By dieting we mean deliberate food restriction that makes you hungry, or sets up cravings for food. This approach to weight loss is counterproductive, because it involves fighting your body, making an enemy of it. If dieting were the answer, all those books, those millions of magazine articles, and the suffering of all those diet addicts would have produced the thinnest nation in the world; it has not.

We do, however, make specific dietary recommendations. There are certain foods that should be avoided because they are particularly dangerous, either because of the metabolic disruption they induce or because they are likely to be loaded with toxins. Other foods will offer specific benefits for PFR victims, and details of these are given in our dietary chapter. But we are not going to treat you as if you were a child who is incapable of learning how much food you should eat. You have to be in control, after all.

The recommendations we make are specifically aimed at helping you overcome your PFR problem. We offer a balanced diet, a way of eating that anyone susceptible to PFR should try to follow throughout his or her life. We believe that it is an eating pattern that will enhance the health and longevity of anyone following its recommendations.

How long will it all take? There is no simple answer. It is likely that the factors that precipitated your PFR built up over a number of years, perhaps on the diet seesaw, following all those "miracle" diets that took you nowhere; or by the slow accumulation of toxins, after pregnancy or through allergies. If you have been overweight for many years, your bones will have thickened to cope with the additional load, and this will take time to reverse. So it all depends on your particular case; there are too many individual factors for precise estimates. One thing is sure, however: the sooner you start, the sooner you will lose that weight.

You will have to accept that without following The Plan you will probably never be able to lose weight fast without making yourself sick. By following it, you will be able to avoid the accumulation of persistent fat in the future, and you will permanently reduce what you already have.

Because of the permanent nature of the change we are aiming for, you should not rush The Plan. Steady, continuous progress, changing to the sort of person you want to be, is the objective. Work on yourself with perseverance and patience. You need to give your body time to readjust its metabolic priorities. A year may seem an impossibly long time, but it's worth it if, at the end of that time, you weigh many pounds less and are sure that you need never put that weight on again. How does that compare with what has happened to you in the last year? Right! So perhaps spending nine months in preparation and three months losing pounds is not such a bad outlook.

What about age? It is true that the younger you are, the quicker your healing and regenerative processes tend to be, but this is balanced by the greater tenacity more mature people generally have. People of any age can lose fat—even persistent fat. Everyone can help their liver and improve their general health. Too often in our culture we are led to believe that health and vitality are found only in the young. Nonsense! With current health trends, age is increasingly irrelevant; the young are suffering all the complaints that used to afflict only the aged. It is true that the older you are, the longer it will probably take, and the harder you will have to work at it.

By improving the metabolic capacity of your body and enhancing healing and detoxification systems, you will become healthier whatever your age. The Plan is designed for people of all ages, so do not be discouraged by thinking you are too old for it.

We are sure that once you start you will quickly feel much better. You will have more energy and interest in life. Your eyes will be clearer, the whites whiter. And your increasing health will mean that you will want to be more physically active. Once this happens, you will know beyond doubt that you are on the right track. As an added bonus, you will be less likely to suffer minor infections and spend less time feeling below par or generally sick.

The first thing you will notice, perhaps within days, is a new glow to your skin. Your color will improve and you will start to look better, even before you start to lose excess fat. Ex-dieters, particularly, will notice the improvement. It is your body starting to reward you for your new regimen of care and attention.

10

The Diet—Innocent Food

You must eat food that, beyond any shadow of doubt, is not guilty of causing you harm. Ideally, this means eating organically produced food. This will probably mean making significant changes in your current eating habits and tossing out many of your assumptions about what is good food and what is not. The essentials of the PFR diet depend on the quality of what you eat.

The primary aim of the PFR diet is to reduce to the absolute minimum the amount of artificial chemicals that enter your liver through the digestive system. To do this, you have to seek pure, innocent food: food that has been subjected to a minimum of interference during its growth and subsequent processing. Eating such food will reduce the load on your detoxifying systems and will also reduce the concentration of chemicals in your blood and tissues.

The secondary aim of the PFR diet is to provide enough of all the nutrients that you need to rebuild your liver. For this you need adequate quantities of the right foods, and we explain which types are important to you. Unfortunately, finding pure food is not simple. As we have seen, ordinary food is a chemical minefield. It is one that has to be negotiated, however, and success in this area could solve the biggest part of your problem. We believe that most PFR, as well as a variety of other metabolic and health problems, can be attributed to eating what amounts to poisonous food.

When you follow the PFR diet, you will be cutting your intake of synthetic additives and pesticide residues to the minimum possible. We realize that most people will not be able to live entirely on additive- and residue-free food, and that everyone will want to eat out occasionally, or indulge in their favorite (banned) foods. However, the closer your diet to the ideal described in this chapter, the faster you will achieve detoxification and increased metabolic capacity, and the faster you will be able to lose that persistent fat.

As you grow accustomed to this way of eating, you will find that you prefer it—and you may well wonder how you put up with synthetically flavored and detextured processed foods for so long. As your body systems improve, you will notice a whole series of benefits accrue from the PFR diet. But that's a general characteristic of all aspects of the escape plan!

AVOIDING ADDITIVES

If you recall the uses to which additives are put, you will already have a very good idea how to avoid them. The rules are quite simple:

1. Good food is food that will go bad.

You should buy fresh food and eat it at its best. If its best lasts a long time, it is usually because it has been treated with preservatives. The exceptions are dried beans, grains, and fruit; these are normally rehydrated (when they can once more go bad easily) before you actually eat them.

2. The best food is the least-processed food.

Obviously, when you pick it off the tree and eat it raw, the processing is minimal. Aim to get food that has had the least done to it. Prepared foods—TV dinners, packaged snacks, bakery goods—are usually heavily processed. Fast-food does not even bear thinking about—and you should never, ever, consider eating it.

It is possible to buy prepared foods that are completely additive-free, and the range is growing with public demand. Your local health-food store is obviously a good source, but more and more supermarkets are stocking such foods. Brands to look for include Walnut Acres, Health Valley, and Pritikin, whose canned vegetarian foods and soups can provide instant hot meals.

Read all the small print on labels carefully. Learn the names of the worst additives, or check those on the products you don't want to give up using. One difficulty is margarine; many brands contain additives that could cause you problems.

Another problem is bread. Bread is—or should be—an excellent food, one that we would wholeheartedly recommend. Unfortunately, it is extremely difficult to get additive-free bread in most places. We have tackled this problem by speaking to a small family bakery, promising a firm order of chemical-free loaves baked from organic flour. We naturally pay more for these loaves, but believe it's worthwhile.

Your baker may assure you that his stone-ground, wholemeal bread is fine—but is it? Even if he doesn't add any chemicals, most flour contains preservatives, and the wheat is fumigated with carbon tetrachloride (the liquid used for dry-cleaning clothes), a known liver poison that lingers in the flour. If you bake your own, of course you know what's going into it. Choose your flour carefully and use fresh or dried yeast, not a "quick" yeast. Another alternative is to buy organic pumpernickel. It's delicious and sealed into airtight packs which will last.

Cheese is another additive problem area; normally, there's no information to guide you, though colors and preservatives are often added. Our advice is to avoid it or cut your consumption very low. Details on which types to choose if you're a cheese-lover come later in this chapter.

Finally, a word about a substance that you may not think of as a food additive: sugar. If you ever drive past a sugar-producing factory, you will see what looks like a huge chemical-processing plant. That's where they make that white chemical we call sugar. Our bodies were never designed to cope with such a substance. Its consumption causes metabolic shock through insulin rebound; one outcome of this is that the body tends to dump white sugar molecules into fat—this is why it is known to be fattening.

Dark brown sugars, maple syrup, and honey are not quite as bad as white sugar, but they can still cause metabolic problems. Avoid them if possible; otherwise restrict your intake to a maximum of two teaspoonfuls per day.

AVOIDING PESTICIDE RESIDUES

Ideally, you should eat only organically produced food. That means food that has been grown with organic fertilizers like compost and manure and that has not been treated with synthetic pesticides, and animals that have been reared naturally. This is food produced as an integral part of the biological life cycle; the waste from natural processes is returned to the soil to enhance its fertility. It is an entirely natural cycle, one that can be sustained indefinitely without synthetic input. It is a method of farming that produces healthy plants and animals and health-enhancing food. Eating natural, organic food usually means preparing your own food at home. If you habitually eat in restaurants and snack bars, you will have to reorganize your life a little.

We are realists, and we know that eating organic food all the time is not possible for most people. Although the network of suppliers is increasing fast, organic food is not available everywhere. You may have to buy in bulk and freeze perishable organic produce when you find it. Your intake of pesticides will be reduced automatically when you follow the PFR diet, but the more of your food that is organically produced, the better.

The first rule of the PFR diet is to totally avoid animal fat and internal organs. Like humans, animals store pesticide and drug residues in their fat and organs such as liver, kidneys, and heart. Unless you have access to organically reared meat, you should not have more than two meat meals per week, with no more than three ounces of meat at each. Never eat organ meats. Avoid meat from all animals that have been intensively reared—particularly veal, pork and bacon products, and chicken. New Zealand lamb is still free-range, so this will be less contaminated. Cook it thoroughly to get rid of as much fat as possible, and skim the fat off the cooking juices before making gravy.

Free-range birds and animals are likely to contain fewer residues. Wild rabbit, wild duck, venison, and, if you are in a country where you can get it, wild boar, can be good food sources. Game from open country should be all right, but avoid pheasants from oversprayed lowland grain fields.

You should eat fish about twice weekly. Fish are an excellent food, because they swim free and are not dosed with any chemicals—although they can pick them up from the sea through pesticide runoff from fields and chemical pollution from industry. Avoid farmed fish, such as trout. Hatchery fish and freshwater fish should be eaten in limited amounts or avoided. Fatty fish such as mackerel, bluefish, and salmon should be eaten no more frequently than once or twice a month and only after visible fat under the skin has been removed. Smaller, younger fish are less contaminated than more mature fish. The level of pollutants in shellfish depends on local conditions in the waters in which the shellfish were caught. Buy all your fish from a good fresh-fish store, preferably not fish in cans or frozen, and never eat "fish sticks." Avoid "smoked" fish, which is usually colored with coal-tar dye. Never take fish-liver oil dietary supplements: fish livers are highly polluted. If you are eating out, fish can be a good choice.

Most dairy produce is polluted with residues, but you can avoid the worst of them by choosing only low-fat forms. Do not eat butter—substitute good-quality cold-pressed oils, such as olive oil and sunflower oil, for cooking. Choose skim milk, low-fat natural yogurt, and low-fat cheeses, such as part-skim ricotta, feta, part-skim mozzarella, farmer, hoop, and pot cheese. Avoid cottage cheese, even if it is low-fat, unless you are sure it does not contain preservatives: the leading brands do. Hain is a good choice. Use goat- or sheep-milk products whenever possible; these are now often available at supermarkets, as well as health-food stores. If you hate goat's milk, do try sheep's—it tastes quite different.

Eggs are included in the PFR diet because they contain vitamins and amino acids that are essential to good liver function. But you must buy free-range: you will get a less polluted egg, and the vitamin levels are much higher. The flavor's much better too! We recommend that you eat between three and seven eggs a week, but do not fry them.

Proteins are important to good liver function, and the least polluted sources are vegetables. Remember that whole grains, nuts, seeds, peas, and beans are good sources of protein, but you have to eat a mixture of them; combine brown rice or other grains with peas, beans, or nuts to get the right balance. Nuts and seeds (particularly sunflower seeds) are very good in salads, or for nibbling. They play an important part in the PFR diet, as we'll explain later.

Fresh vegetables complement vegetable protein foods, and together these form the core of the PFR diet. You should try to eat a salad every day because cooking removes valuable nutrients from many vegetables. Your salads should contain a handful of sprouted beans, grains, or seeds, as well as the more familiar leaves, roots, and vegetable fruits. You will be producing these sprouts yourself, in the kitchen cupboard or other dark spot, because that way you can be sure of an unpolluted source of essential, health-giving nutrients every day.

For those who have not tried sprouting, here's how you start. Buy some mung beans from your local health-food store. Put a tablespoon of them in a wide-mouthed jar. Cover them with plenty of boiled water, cooled down to lukewarm. Put the jar in a warm, dark place. After twenty-four hours, pour off the water and rinse your beans thoroughly. Then, every twelve hours or so, rinse the sprouting beans under the tap, draining off all the water you can and returning them to the jar. After three days or so, your beans will have sprouts about an inch and a half long, and fresh green leaves just showing. Put the jar on your windowsill for a day. Now your sprouts are ready to eat—preferably raw, but lightly stir-fried if you must cook them. You will find that the tablespoon of beans you started with has produced two handfuls of sprouts—enough for you for two days! It's the cheapest form of food we know, as well as one of the most nutritious.

The same basic method can be used for such grains as wheat and rye, for sunflower seeds, and for other types of beans. More details are given in Leslie and Susannah Kenton's excellent book *Raw Energy*. It's well worth buying for its original salad ideas alone—and it will prove very useful to you when you're applying the rules of the PFR diet to your life.

Most of your food—including the beans and seeds you'll need for sprouting—will come from your local health-food store. But be wary, they can also carry esoteric junk in the name of health, or imports of dubious origin. Study the label and question the staff carefully to ensure that you are getting unsprayed, organically grown food whenever possible, because there are still comparatively few stores that sell only organic produce.

Some supermarkets are beginning to stock organic and health-food products. Encourage them by asking for food they do not yet have on the shelves. Again, read labels carefully. And avoid those supermarkets that find it necessary to pollute their entire premises with chemical cleaners in the name of hygiene. It is totally unnecessary and only adds to your problem. (We watched the inside of a fully stocked cheese cabinet being sprayed with "cleanser"! Not the best way to treat food.)

Fresh produce has no guarantee of purity, and you will have to rely on the integrity of the store or market. If it is sold as "organic," it should contain no pesticide residues. But remember, "health foods" are no more likely to be pesticide-free than any others, unless they are specifically marked as such.

Strangely enough, your best guarantee may be things that used to be thought of as pests. If there are greenflies on the lettuce, the odd caterpillar in the cabbage, or even a maggot in an apple, you can be fairly sure that, if it is safe for them, it is safe for you. Try looking upon these humble creatures as the modern equivalent of the miner's canary. While the canary sang in the pit, the men knew they were safe from poisonous gas. Where insects are happy, you are safe; where they are being poisoned, so are you.

Luckily there are certain old, established brands whose food has managed to retain its integrity. Again, their products may not always be 100 percent organic, but the label will state this where it is the case. You should make a note of the names, ask for their produce as often as possible, and buy them as a matter of course.

Look for Erewhon Trading Company, Mountain Ark Trading

Company, and Autumn Harvest Natural Foods. Organic flours are available from various millers; we recommend Arrowhead Mills whole wheat flour—it makes the most delicious bread. If you have difficulty in finding these brands, the addresses of these firms are in Appendix 3; a self-addressed envelope with your inquiry would probably be appreciated.

Appendix 3 also gives a list of organic suppliers. More are springing up all the time, so do not assume you cannot get organic food just because we have not included a shop in your area in the list. Further information is available in the *East West Journal* (P.O. Box 1200, Brookline, MA 02147).

While things are getting better, it is true that most of us are not able to obtain enough organic food to meet all our needs. So here are some tips that may help.

Have you seriously thought about growing more of your own food? Any garden can support salad crops, and you get them totally fresh and crisp. Lettuces and radishes are the easiest to grow, and fruits such as strawberries need very little attention. You can also eat any part of the nasturtium plant—use the leaves and flowers in salads and pickle the seeds to eat with your fish.

The important thing to remember is that you must maintain a very high level of organic material in the soil, especially if you live in a city. Without this material, you will not be able to produce nourishing crops. If you are anywhere near a road and there is not enough organic material in the soil, your crops could contain lead from car exhausts. Start a compost heap, collect leaf mold, and dig in manure to build high levels of fertility. Many books are available on the subject.

If you have some garden space, you can grow enough fresh food to feed a family for most of the year. This may mean that you spend some Sunday hours as we do, working the soil, but it is a very relaxing and satisfying way of spending time. And use hand tools. Do not join the feeble, powered-everything crowd, who pollute with fumes and noise. You will be getting more exercise and losing weight.

If you don't enjoy gardening, and there isn't a good food store near you, why not think about opening a health-food store? Many of the big alternative-food co-ops and stores started just like this. Try an ad in the local newspaper to find others who might be interested in joining forces with you.

If none of these suggestions is feasible, you will need to protect yourself as best you can by choosing food that is least likely to be polluted with pesticides. Here are some guidelines:

1. Avoid frozen and canned food wherever possible. The processors demand produce that looks absolutely perfect, and the farmers therefore spray more thoroughly.

2. Always peel or thoroughly scrape potatoes; they not only are sprayed repeatedly during growing, but are usually treated after harvesting with chemicals that prevent sprouting.

3. Buy "new" potatoes, carrots, and other vegetables when you have a choice. Select early crops, rather than stored produce. They are less likely to have been sprayed with growth inhibitors.

4. Never buy bright-colored dried fruit; the color is the result of preservatives. Pick brownish apricots and sun-dried, oil-free raisins.

5. Produce commercially grown in the U.S. may not be the best choice for low-residue foods. If you have a choice, buy organic produce from sources that do not use chemicals. It may be wise to avoid Chilean and Mexican produce. You can choose not to eat imported commodities; when something is produced far away and has to be fumigated, you are going to get higher pesticide residues.

Now that you know how to avoid the chemicals that will tend to put a load on your liver, you will need to know about the other side of the diet: the specific nutrients that will help you escape from the PFR Syndrome.

The nutrients described below are essential to The Plan. You must not skimp on the foods that contain them. While you do not have to eat all the foods in each group (Tables 1 to 4 below), you should make sure you do have some of them every day.

Do not imagine you can get away with taking supplements instead; your body may not respond to a synthetic nutrient and could even treat it as yet another toxic additive in your diet!

Liver—as you might guess—is a rich source of many of the nutrients you will need. Unfortunately, it is also a concentrated source of all the poisons to which the animal has been exposed. If you can get naturally reared, organic liver, it will be beneficial; but the product from the local butcher or supermarket is likely to be harmful, and you should not eat it.

Iron is crucial for effective detoxification. It is used in one of the liver's metabolic cycles. Sources are given in Table 1, below. If you avoid drinking tea and coffee, this will increase the amount of iron your body can take up from your food. Avoiding food additives also improves your iron uptake, so if you have tended to be anemic in the past, the PFR diet should remedy the problem.

Other minerals, including selenium and zinc, are also involved in the metabolism of potentially toxic substances and are necessary for recovery and healing. But you are most unlikely to require special mineral supplements, because the diet we recommend should provide adequate quantities. Processed food, grown with chemical fertilizers that provide only a narrow range of minerals and prepared in ways that deplete it of nutrients, is deficient in many trace elements; in contrast, organ-

Table 1. Foods Rich in Iron

Vegetable sources

broccoli	lima beans	radishes
butter beans	mung beans	spinach
lentils	parsley	watercress
leeks	peas	

Fruit sources

avocados	dried apricots	prunes
blueberries	dried currants	raisins
cranberries	dried figs	raspberries
	loganberries	strawberries

Other good sources
nuts (except chestnuts)
dark-colored meat

Table 2. Foods Rich in Folic Acid

Vegetable sources

beets	cabbage	lettuce
broccoli	chicory	other brassicas (raw)
brussels sprouts	corn	scallions
		watercress

Fruit sources

avocados	melons (all types)	oranges	tomatoes

Other good sources

almonds	free-range eggs	walnuts

ically produced food contains a good balance. The selenium you need comes primarily from free-range eggs and organic whole grains, while zinc is plentiful in nuts (particularly brazils), seeds, and grains.

Folic acid, one of the B-group vitamins, is essential for building new liver tissue and to replace cells throughout the body. Sources are in Table 2.

Vitamin C is necessary for healing. Table 3 lists good sources. Unfortunately vitamin C disappears from foods with storage, and the quantity available from most sources falls in winter. This is when you will be relying on bean and grain sprouts— you should eat more in the winter months. Sprouts also contain other vitamins and trace minerals that will help you escape from PFR: the sprouting process increases the quantity available many times.

The amino acids cysteine and methionine are absolutely essential to your success. Cysteine is denatured by cooking, so you must incorporate some raw sources into your diet every day. Brazil nuts are exceptionally rich in both these amino acids, but you must be sure they are fresh. Other sources are given in Table 4.

Table 3. Foods Rich in Vitamin C

Vegetable sources

asparagus	cauliflower	potatoes—the newer the better
bean sprouts	kale	radishes
brussels sprouts	mint	sweet potatoes
cabbage	parsley	watercress

Fruit sources

all berry fruits (blueberries, cranberries, raspberries, strawberries, etc.)	fresh pineapple
	guavas
	honeydew melon
	mangoes
cantaloupe	papaya
citrus fruit (grapefruit, lemons, limes, oranges, tangerines, etc.)	tomatoes

Table 4. Foods Rich in Cysteine and/or Methionine

eggs	corn
fish	millet
	rice
brazil nuts	sunflower seeds
cashew nuts	wheat
walnuts	

APPLYING THE PRINCIPLES OF THE PFR DIET

These are the rules you must follow:

1. Forget everything you have ever thought about dieting.

It is almost certain to be just the kind of psychological baggage that will hinder your escape from the PFR Syndrome. Leave it behind.

2. You must be absolutely sure that you eat enough food.

Your body has a lot of work to do, both in detoxifying and in rebuilding your liver. It will not be able to cope if you keep it short of fuel. Eat plenty of the foods in the preceding tables!

3. Forget about your weight—look at your shape.

You may find that the quantities of food we recommend are greater than you have been used to eating, and you may fear putting on weight. This is a possibility in the short term, while you are rebuilding your liver. Accept this without worrying. You will find that a higher level of metabolic health will mean that you have more energy, and you will start to burn more food. If you have been accustomed to restricting your food intake, your metabolic rate will be depressed. Eat more of the right foods, follow The Plan, and your metabolic rate will increase.

The PFR escape plan calls for two different meal schedules. You'll start with Schedule I, and you may need to stay with this indefinitely. Certainly you should continue on Schedule I for the first two stages of The Plan (detoxification, and mobilizing your metabolism). It requires that you eat many small meals each day and nibble whenever you're hungry. Forget about avoiding between-meal snacks; have as many as you want. But always choose the foods that are recommended in the tables above.

Schedule II is for those who have mobilized their metabolism, rebuilt their liver, and are ready to go on and increase the rate at which toxins stored in body fat are processed. It is to be used with the activity regimen described in the final stages of The Plan. It is designed to deplete your liver stores and build them up again on a cyclic basis, so it calls for just one main meal a day and periods of fasting or very light eating at other times. If you have passed middle age, one meal a day is not for you; older people, roughly those fifty-five and over (but allow for individual variability), should not cut down to fewer than three meals a day.

Our week-by-week action plan (Chapter 13) will explain exactly when you should consider changing from Schedule I to

Table 5. YES Foods

These are your staple foods, and they should be eaten every day. If you are allergic to any particular types, substitute others from the same group.

Food type VEGETABLES	Varieties	Cooking method	Quantity per day	Comments
Brassicas	broccoli, cauliflower, cabbage, brussels sprouts, kale	raw or steamed	as much as you like	
Green salad	any fresh vegetables, homegrown if possible	raw	as much as you like	watercress recommended
Legumes	all peas and beans	lightly boiled	as much as you like	
	butter beans, lentils, lima beans, red beans	boiled or in soups	1 cup cooked	soak and boil hard
Roots	potatoes	boiled or baked	8–14 oz	new, if available
	carrots, beets, rutabagas, turnips, sweet potatoes, etc.	raw or boiled	as much as you like	
Sprouts	bean, seed, or grain	raw or stir-fried	1 handful	homegrown
Other vegetables	leeks, onions, etc.	as desired	as desired	

MISCELLANEOUS PROTEIN SOURCES

Eggs	free-range	not fried	1	
Yogurt	natural, goat- or sheep-milk		5 oz	
Fish	fresh, not smoked	any	4–8 oz	
Tuna	in brine			
Nuts	cashews, brazils, walnuts, almonds	raw	2 oz	
Seeds	sunflower, pumpkin	raw or sprouted	2 oz	as a snack, or in salads

FRUIT

Any fresh fruit		raw	½ to 1 lb	soft fruit recommended, avoid citrus peel
Dried fruit	only unsulphured fruit	raw or boiled	1–2 oz	delicious with yogurt

GRAINS

Brown rice		boiled	as desired	
Rolled oats		granola or porridge	1–2 oz	
Wheat/rye		bread, pasta	2–4 big slices as desired	whole grain

Table 5. YES Foods

Food type	Varieties	Cooking method	Quantity per day	Comments
OIL	olive, sunflower, or wheat germ	for cooking and salads	as required	cold-pressed
SEASONINGS				
Salt	sea salt		use sparingly	
	pepper, spices, herbs		as desired	
	tahini		as desired	
	tamari soy sauce		as desired	
	lemon juice, cider vinegar		as desired	avoid preservatives

Table 6. PERHAPS Foods

Food type	Varieties	Cooking method	Quantity per day	Comments
Milk	skim milk, goats' milk	as required	max. ½ pint	choose goats' or sheeps' milk
Cheese	low-fat cheeses		max. 2 oz	
Meat	poultry or game	as desired	3 oz per day (but not every day)	free-range
	lamb	remove fat	3 oz weekly	New Zealand
	lamb's liver	broiled or braised	3 oz	organic only
Breakfast cereals	Nutragrain, Grapenuts, Shredded Wheat, Puffed Wheat, other sugar-free cereals		normal helping	organic oats preferable
Peanuts			2 oz weekly	unsalted and unflavored

Table 7. NO Foods

Avoid these as far as possible—although if you find organic or additive-free varieties, they will be fine.

Food	Varieties	Comments
Breakfast cereals	sweetened varieties, corn flakes, bran cereals, etc.	contain sugar, additives
Dairy produce	whole cows' milk, cream, full-fat cheeses	residues in fat
	fruit/nut yogurt	contains sugar, additives
	ice cream	contains sugar, additives
Desserts, pastries, candy, jams	commercially prepared products	contain sugar, additives, except Walnut Acres jams—but still max. 1 tsp.
Flour products	cookies, cakes, crackers	contain sugar, additives
	white bread	contains bleach, additives
Meat	beef, pork, veal, chicken, turkey, etc.	residues in fat
Sauces and dressings (including those integrated into foods, such as baked beans, pasta, etc.)	commercially prepared products	contain additives, sugar

Schedule II. Both schedules demand that you eat the same basic foods, but the balance is changed as you progress. So the first thing you need to know is what foods to eat, and in what quantities.

We cannot give strict rules on quantities. As we have already emphasized, there is tremendous individual variation in food needs, and you will have to judge for yourself when you have had enough. Just remember the second rule: always eat enough food! This is easier when you follow the PFR diet because you will not be confusing your body with processed foods, which don't provide the signals that tell you when you've had what you need.

We have divided the foods into YES, PERHAPS, and NO. You will be relying on the YES group primarily. PERHAPS foods are to be eaten with caution; they are not essential, and you should not have large quantities of them. You should aim to avoid NO foods completely, as they are likely to contain chemicals that will interfere with your progress.

These lists are not comprehensive—we could not make them so. They are intended as a guide, and you will have to work out which group other foodstuffs would fall into by referring to the lists and the text above.

CREATING MENUS: SCHEDULE I

The menus suggested below are, once again, offered as a guide. You do not need to stick to them, if you can think of ways you'd prefer to make your YES Foods into everyday meals.

When you wake up

Herb tea, bottled spring water, or fruit juice diluted with an equal amount of water.

Breakfast

½ grapefruit (no sugar)

Bowl of organic hot cereal (no milk or sugar). We make cereal for two with 1 cup organic breakfast oats, 2½ cups water, ½ level tsp. sea salt, 1 tsp. organic oat or wheat bran. It's delicious on its own—nothing needs to be added!

or

Small bowl organic granola with skimmed milk or yogurt

or

Stewed dried fruit, with organic wheat germ and yogurt

or

Boiled or poached egg with whole grain toast

Coffee Break (midmorning snack)

1 slice whole grain bread with margarine, olive oil, or tahini

or

Sunflower seeds and fresh fruit

or

Natural yogurt

Lunch

Sprouted seed and fresh vegetable salad with whole grain bread or pumpernickel

or

Split-pea or lentil soup with whole grain croutons

or

Brown rice with stir-fried vegetables

Midafternoon Snack

Fresh fruit and nuts or seeds

Pumpernickel bread with raw sprouts

Dinner

Baked or broiled fish with vegetables

or

Boiled egg with potatoes and salad

or

Free-range poultry with baked potato and vegetables or salad

or

Chili-flavored beans with rice and salad

or

Organic, whole wheat pasta with tahini and vegetable sauce, seafood sauce, or tomato sauce, with 1 oz finely grated Gouda or mozzarella cheese

or

Cabbage leaves, pepper, eggplant, or young zucchini, stuffed with rice, nuts, tomatoes, and shallots (Greek recipes are very good—but halve the quantity of oil!)

or

Bean and vegetable stew

Fresh fruit

GENERAL COMMENTS

You should make sure you have at least one serving of fresh salad every day. Add bean, grain, and seed sprouts to your salads for their high vitamin content.

Vary your salads with vegetables you normally cook—such as grated young turnips (delicious with chopped apricots and walnuts), or raw zucchini, or flowers such as marigolds and nasturtiums from the garden. Make dressings with natural yogurt and herbs, cold-pressed oil (watch for preservatives!), and lemon juice, avocado, and wine vinegar pureed in a food processor—*Raw Energy* (see References, p. 209) has many imaginative suggestions.

Try going Chinese: stir-fry cashew nuts with finely chopped vegetables in a little oil; season with tamari or another naturally fermented soy sauce. Other cultures—both Eastern and Near Eastern—have traditions of eating in ways that will fit in well with your PFR diet.

Potential problems:

You're desperate for a cookie, but you know they're forbidden. . . . Have a rice cake; buy a sugar-free brand, such as Chico-San or Spiral.

You passionately want something sweet—like chocolate. . . . Try carob-coated raisins (not too many), or chew a couple of dried figs. Avoid the sweetened, supermarket version—we can't imagine why anyone would want to make figs even sweeter than they are!

You long for your favorite junk snack. This one can be more difficult because you may be addicted or allergic to the additives and sugar in processed foods. They give your metabolism a jolt like that produced by addictive drugs. The mechanism is similar; these substances pervert your metabolic processes, and just as withdrawal from drugs can be difficult, so can withdrawal from processed foods, for those who have become dependent on them. Recognize your addiction for what it is—and acknowledge that it could be the major cause of your PFR problem. Do not give in: search determinedly for additive-free substitutes, and don't allow yourself to go hungry. Hunger could undermine your willpower.

Gradually remove all temptation of this sort from your house. Wean your family off it; they will benefit too. After a while, you will find such foods taste just as revolting as they are. Nobody will be able to pass off to you any synthetic imitations of real, flavorful food anymore!

SCHEDULE II

By the time you get this far, you will be totally accustomed to eating on the PFR diet. The changes you will be making now are not fundamental; it's a question of changing the balance of your diet.

On Schedule II, you will be very physically active, and you will want to eat more food. Do not increase your consumption of protein foods such as fish, eggs, and nuts; choose more complex carbohydrates—particularly grains and root vegetables.

Breakfast
Piece of fruit
Small bowl hot cereal or granola
Midmorning Snack
1 cup coffee if desired
Lunch
As Schedule I
Midafternoon Snack
2 slices whole grain bread with fresh sprouts or salad vegetables
Piece of fresh fruit
Sunflower seeds or nuts
Dinner
Lentil, split pea, or vegetable soup
or
Melon, grapefruit, or avocado
Main course as Schedule I, but double portions of potato, rice, pasta, bean and vegetable stew
Fresh and/or dried stewed fruit, or baked apple stuffed with dried fruit and 1 tsp. honey, with yogurt

or

Fruit pie or additive-free dessert (sweetened with concentrated apple juice or dried fruit)

Rice cakes, pumpernickel or other bread, with 1 oz low-fat cheese if desired

DRINK (SCHEDULE I AND II)

Now that you have the rules for eating, you will be wondering what to wash it down with. There's no point in detoxifying one part of your intake and ruining the effect by pouring in liquid hazards!

The most important rule is that you drink enough water. Drink just as much of this as you like, at any time of the day. Never restrict your liquid intake: this will interfere with detoxification.

Sensible people stick to those drinks that will help their systems rather than add to the load on them. Pure spring water sold in glass bottles (such as Perrier) is good for your liver and digestion, and delicious too.

Fresh fruit and vegetable juices (not fruit drinks) are also excellent. But read the labels—drinks often contain junk. Look for purity. Citrus juices contain valuable vitamin C, necessary for healing and detoxification, and carrot juice is rich in vitamin A. Cranberry juice is used to acidify urea in case of kidney or bladder infection. It is possible to get organic fruit juice; check the labels on bottles in your local health-food store, and stock up with the types you prefer. Walnut Acres juices are uncontaminated, but this is not the only brand you may find. Dilute juices half-and-half with water for a more refreshing drink.

Coffee, tea, and chocolate may cause problems and can interfere with efforts to detoxify your body and improve liver function. You would be wise to give up drinking them and substitute herb teas. Lime-flower, camomile, marigold, and mint teas may be particularly helpful. When you reach Schedule II, you may be able to drink one or two cups of ordinary tea and/or coffee a day without harming your progress, but don't let the quantities build up.

Hazards: soft drinks and colas—low-calorie or otherwise— are completely banned. PFR victims may be particularly vulnerable to such products. These concoctions of colors, flavorings, and sweeteners merely add to your chemical load. The same goes for milkshakes. Don't touch them!

Milk, and dairy products generally, should be used only minimally. Contaminated animal fats are concentrated in most dairy products. Strawberries, yes; cream—no! And don't replace milk with nondairy creamer—it's a totally unnatural, chemical product. Avoid drinking tea and coffee, and you'll rarely want milk. What milk you do use should be skim, or goat's milk.

Water from the faucet is assumed to be safe, but it can contain hazardous chemical residues. Reports of contaminated ground water increase yearly. Water filters are readily available; they make your water a refreshing drink once more. Ask your dealer for one that includes either ion-exchange resin plus an activated charcoal filter, or two columns of different ion-exchange resins.

You will realize that alcohol is likely to pose particular problems for PFR sufferers. It is well known that alcohol attacks the liver and that alcoholics tend to die of liver disease. Obviously, your best choice is to avoid all alcohol, at least until you are established on Stage Three of The Plan. Some will have already made this decision, having observed that alcohol makes them sick.

If you will not abstain from alcohol, the next best solution is to choose the least hazardous forms and drink only occasionally, and then in moderation. The old Scots habit of the "wee dram"—one small whiskey—each night has been statistically demonstrated to be a healthy one. Insist on traditional quality and flavor; brewers and distillers are experimenting with product development, and the results of their innovation are increasingly artificial.

Rapidly produced, cheap forms of alcoholic drink will contain not only alcohols of various types, but a whole range of other substances, such as sulfites. Large-scale brewing and wine making are now chemically controlled processes, and residues remain in the end product.

Good-quality wines, especially the Four Chimneys Farm wine*

---

* Four Chimneys Farm Winery, Himrod-on-Seneca, New York 14842.

and French "biologique" wines, produced without the use of chemicals in growing or fermentation, are likely to cause your body fewer problems than the less expensive ones. White wine, in general, is more easily metabolized than red wine.

If you have noticed that you tend to get a particularly nasty hangover after certain drinks, avoid those completely.

If you do have a few drinks at a celebration, you should help your liver to cope with the load as quickly and efficiently as possible. Take plenty of water or pure fruit juice between alcoholic drinks, and go for a brisk walk or dance energetically for at least twenty minutes to burn up the alcohol. A brisk walk home, instead of a car ride, could have the same effect. The worst thing to do is to sit or stand around drinking, cocktail-party style, and then go to sleep. Your efforts to improve liver function will receive a severe setback every time you allow this to happen.

Finally, if you are offered a slice of lemon with your drink, refuse it. The peel will almost certainly be polluted with fungicides that will dissolve in your drink. Some of those sprayed on citrus fruits are the most hazardous in common use. As for "cocktail cherries" . . . you just have to look at the color of those things to know they won't do you any good at all. No thanks!

11

Your Environment

While chemicals in food, drink, and medicines are most likely to cause PFR problems, for some people environmental toxins may be more critical. But because we live in an environment that abounds in artificial chemicals, we take most of the products involved for granted, and few people think about the way the everyday chemicals they encounter may affect them. However, toxins reach your liver and your fat stores through a variety of other routes besides the food and drink you consume. They will add to your personal loading and exacerbate the problem. As a PFR victim, you can be sure only by minimizing your exposure to all sources of potential problems.

At first sight this may seem extreme. But does it make sense to clean up your food and drink intake, while ignoring your immediate environment? You will be beginning to think of food and drink in a different way, wondering how we could allow the manufacturers to behave as they do; you have to see your environment in the same way. Can you expect to be healthy and beautiful if all around you industrial products are degrading and contaminating the space you occupy? You are seeing yourself with new eyes; extend your new vision to the world around you.

In addition to food additives, drugs, and pesticides, the

chemical industry produces a vast range of substances that end up in our environment, from household cleansers, polishes, and sprays to personal products from deodorizers to perfumes, and many office and industrial products. For PFR victims, it is ironic that they may be persuaded to buy things to pollute their environment by being led to believe that such products are highly desirable, if not indispensable.

Because of our individual differences in metabolism, it is not possible to predict which sources will be most important for everybody; you will be relatively more sensitive to one group of chemicals, less affected by another. With your growing knowledge of yourself and your growing understanding of the nature of the problem, you may begin to identify particular groups that adversely affect you.

In this chapter, we explain how and where you can identify some of the most common sources of environmental toxins. The first part concerns your home—and we predict that you will be shocked to discover just how many toxic threats it contains!

Complete the questionnaire below to find out.

Arm yourself with a notepad and pen, put on some old clothes, and set off on the hunt. (Kids and other members of the household can join in; it could be made into a good rainy-afternoon game!)

1. Count all the aerosol sprays in your home.
   a. Check your personal items—hairsprays, deodorants, medicines, shaving cream, etc. How many aerosol cans are there?
   b. Now check fabric-care sprays, such as starch, dry-cleaning, and waterproofing products. How many of these?
   c. How many spray polishes and cleaners?
   d. How many spray paints, varnishes, and dyes?
   e. How many cans of air freshener or room deodorizer?
   f. How many cans of fly spray, pet flea spray, household insecticide spray?
   g. Do you use any other sprays in the kitchen—e.g., coatings for cooking pots? How many of these?

2. Do you use laundry powder or liquid that contains enzymes, those biological types?

3. Do you use products that leave your clothes perfumed (including fabric conditioners)?

4. a. Do you regularly wear dry-cleaned clothes?
   b. Does your partner wear dry-cleaned clothes?
   c. Are any of your furnishings dry-cleaned?

5. Do you use long-lasting or block deodorizers (e.g., in the bathroom or kitchen)? Check your toilet paper—we recently bought, in error, some perfumed rolls that made us sneeze!

6. Do you use long-lasting insecticides (Black Flag Professional Power Ant or Roach Killer or D-Con Double Powder)?

7. Do you use insecticidal pet shampoo, or does your pet wear a flea collar?

8. Do you use strong-smelling glues (such as Weldwood's Contact Cement) in the house?

9. Is there any new paint in the house (painted within the past six weeks)?

10. Do you have formaldehyde-urea foam insulation in the walls of your home?

11. Has the wood in your home been treated with a preservative within the past year?

12. Do you have furniture with flexible plastic covers?

13. Do you have flexible plastic clothing, shower curtains, tablecloths, etc?

Now check outside: the garage, garden shed, and car.

14. Do you have a new car?

15. Do you use cellulose (acetate- or nitrate-based) paints?

16. Do you use paint or varnish strippers?

17. Is there an air freshener in your car?

18. Do you use pesticides in the garden?

Finally, back in the house, check your heating and cooking facilities.

19. Do you have gas heaters or a gas stove?

20. Do you use kerosene or bottled gas heaters?

Now check your chemical contaminant rating:

Question 1. All aerosol sprays are capable of causing problems. Count 1 for each can you find.

Question 2. Add 5 for biological laundry detergent.

Question 3. Occasional use: add 2; regular use: add 5.

Question 4a. Add 2 for each day in the past two weeks when you wore clothes dry-cleaned within the month.

4b. Add 1 for each day your partner wore recently dry-cleaned clothes in the past two weeks.

4c. Add 2 per item of furniture, carpets, or curtains dry-cleaned within the past 6 months.

Question 5. Add 2 per item.

Question 6. Add 5 per item.

Question 7. Add 2 per flea collar, 2 for each use of shampoo within the past 6 weeks.

Question 8. Add 4 for each use within the past 6 weeks.

Question 9. Add 4 for each room repainted within past 6 weeks; plus 4, if you did the painting.

Question 10. Add 10 if yes.

Question 11. Add 20 if yes.

Question 12. Add 10 for furniture less than 1 year old; 2 per item more than 1 year old. (Count only flexible coverings.)

Question 13. Add 4 per item less than 1 year old, 2 per item over 1 year old.

Question 14. Add 4 for a car less than 1 year old.

Question 15. Add 6 for each use within the past 6 weeks.

Question 16. Add 6 for each use within the past 6 weeks.

Question 17. Add 2 if yes.

Question 18. Add 2 for each type.

Question 19. Add 20 if you can smell gas anywhere in the house.

And whether or not you can smell gas, add 2 for every gas heating or cooking appliance.

Question 20. Add 2 for every bottled gas or kerosene heater.

Now check your rating:

Over 140

Your home is heavily contaminated with chemicals. Check which sources are most significant and start working immediately on eliminating them. Specific advice comes later in this chapter.

You are overanxious about dirt, pests, and natural smells. Perhaps you take undue notice of the heavy advertising that is designed to make you buy, buy, buy? Remember that a chemical "fresh" smell is likely to be damaging to your health and figure, and use your nose to judge the hazard. Anything you can smell is present in the air you breathe, and it goes straight into your bloodstream from the membranes of your nose and lungs.

A chemically coated surface may be germ-free, and it may look good—but that doesn't make it clean or healthy.

If you've been doing a lot of painting and house renovation, you will have been exposed to a heavy chemical load, and you may not be willing to stop the work yet. Protect yourself by keeping the house, car, garage, or shed very well ventilated. Leave all the doors and windows open as much as you can; let fresh air waft the poisons away.

90 to 140

The chemical contamination level of your home is high and is likely to cause you problems, if you are at all susceptible. Probably you have a heavy load from some sources and little trouble with others. Think about why you use so many chemicals: is it convenience, ignorance of their dangers, an overconscientious attitude to cleaning and polishing?

Now that you've been alerted to the major sources of chemical contaminants in your home environment, you will be more aware of them. Throw away as many as you can, stop using others, go back to methods of cleaning that your grandmother might have used.

40 to 90

You are not an excessive user of chemicals, but you still have more sources of contamination in your home than you really need. Whether they prove a problem to you depends on your personal sensitivity; you might be reacting very badly to particular sources, so that the limited range in your home still represents too much for your detoxifying systems.

Focus on any products that make you sneeze or feel sick in any way, and get rid of them. Then gradually reduce your use of other potential sources of problems.

Under 40

The level of contamination in your home is well below average, and it may not represent a problem for you unless you are sensitive to particular sources.

If, however, you suffer from any allergies, especially hayfever or asthma, you will need to look critically at every single item that contaminates the air you breathe. The chances are that you can get rid of most of them without much difficulty.

All those who suffer from persistent fat or any allergic problems should do their very best to reduce their household pollution score to 20 or less.

Here are some tips:

Washing and Cleaning

A generation ago, most of the cleaning products we use now had not been invented. They come from the enormous petrochemical industry, where new compounds are developed all the time and sold to the public with clever marketing that is designed to exploit our fears of "dirt," "germs," and social unacceptability.

For many people, probably including you, the contamination they substitute in order to remove these hazards is far worse than the original problem. They are sold by appealing to implied social values; to understand this problem, you may have to shake out some more unwanted psychological baggage.

Does a pair of grass-stained shorts on your child really mean you are a bad mother, as the detergent advertisements imply?

Surely your first priority is to keep your children fit and well—
not glazed and gleaming, subjected to potential poisons for the
ultimate benefit of the chemical industry. Bright, white
washing comes second after health. Be clean without being
obsessive.

Never have anything dry-cleaned if you can wash it. Often you
can ignore labels on clothing that say "dry clean only." In our
experience, hand washing with a gentle liquid product or pure
soap rarely does any damage; most warnings are quite unnecessary. Test a small part where it won't matter if the color runs,
to see if it can actually stand washing. It's also less expensive
than dry cleaning.

If clothes really must be dry-cleaned, don't do it more often
than is absolutely necessary, and then hang them outside to air
for as long as possible before you put them away or wear them.
And when you're choosing clothes or furnishings, pick those
that can be washed. Nobody needs to be exposed to poisonous
fumes from dry-cleaning solvents.

Dry-cleaning fluids—including those you use at home—are
known to cause liver problems. Sensitive people have been
shown to have high levels of these chemicals in their blood
after wearing, or being close to, dry-cleaned clothes or
furnishings.

On Cleaning Generally

For you the answer to smells and odors is not in bottles or
sprays. Use old-fashioned soap and water, rediscover washing
soda, use natural perfumes wherever you can. If you have body-
odor problems, you will find as you become healthier and less
contaminated that you will naturally leave much of this problem behind. It may be caused by the chemicals you are using to
solve it!

For your home, a damp cloth and a vacuum cleaner will cope
with almost everything.

When replacing clothes, fabrics, and furnishings, choose materials that do not require complicated cleaning and care routines.

One Final Word on Cleaning

Rinse everything thoroughly. Never add anything to the final rinsing water (except such natural products as lemon juice or vinegar for brightness). And that applies to you, as well as to your dishwashing and laundry. You will not benefit from having any part of yourself or your environment covered with a chemical film—even if it does give a nice shine.

A general avoidance of all perfumes except those from known, natural sources is wise. Avoid synthetically perfumed cosmetics, soaps, and cleaning products; instead, make your house smell sweet with plants, rose petals, and herbs like lavender. Handle cut flowers—especially long-lasting ones such as chrysanthemums—with care; some have such high levels of pesticide on them that they have poisoned florists!

Plastic fabrics and fabric coatings are hazardous, because the chemicals used to make them flexible slowly evaporate into the air. When they've finally gone and the product is safe, it's stiff and liable to tear—which is when we throw it away!

One of the most potentially dangerous plastics is PVC. The chemical that leaches out of it is vinyl chloride, which is known to cause cancer and liver disease. PVC is used in soft plastic food containers and many other items, such as plastic baby pants. The ideal option would be to avoid everything made of flexible plastic.

The familiar smell of a new car is the smell of plasticizers that evaporate from seat coverings and other interior furnishings. If you buy a new car, leave all the doors open as often as possible, especially in warm weather. Drive with the windows open until the smell disappears.

Plastics come in a great many forms. We cannot hope to give a complete list here. Let your nose be your guide when choosing household or other goods that might be capable of adding to your personal pollution level: avoid anything that has more than the slightest plastic smell. And never, never burn plastic products or breathe the fumes from burning plastic.

If you are surrounded by plastic derivatives that fill your air with unavoidable fumes, you may have a serious problem. Some people living in houses or mobile homes with formaldehyde-urea foam insulation have been forced to move or have the insulation removed because they were unable to enjoy a healthy life when they were breathing formaldehyde every day. If you suspect this to be at the root of your problem, you could check your suspicions by leaving your home for a couple of weeks—for a complete change of environment—to see if your condition improves. This isn't a perfect test by any means, but it might give you an insight into your situation.

People living in gas-heated homes, or cooking on gas stoves, have a similar problem. Many allergy sufferers have had all their gas appliances removed and report a considerable improvement in their condition. But this is an expensive choice to make, and you will want to be sure that gas is a serious problem for you before you do it. First make sure any slight leaks are fixed so that you cannot smell gas at any time. Then, if you still suspect problems, we suggest that you get the gas company to switch your gas off for a few weeks in the summer, while you rely on electric appliances. If you are sensitive to gas, you should notice a marked change in the way you feel within a few days.

We would advise all those who suffer from persistent fat, or who have any reason to believe their bodies do not cope well with chemicals, to try to avoid using gas. Bear this in mind when you choose a new home.

Getting Rid of Insects without Using Chemicals

Avoiding chemicals can have some potentially annoying consequences. One is the need to adjust to an environment that other creatures can share—a good sign because it is life-supporting.

If flies are not being killed by poisons in the air in your home, then they do tend to buzz around the room! And when you take the flea collar off your pet and throw away the pest spray, you are liable to face flea problems. How do you cope?

There is the possibility of changing your own perception a little. We are much less tolerant of other life-forms now that we can practice mass-murder by poison. Perhaps the odd insect in the home is not so dreadful?

Other ways of dealing with pests are available, even if they are not as thorough as chemicals can be. The vacuum cleaner was responsible for banishing the human flea from our homes; it is still the most potent weapon. Used frequently, especially where your pet sleeps, it will keep the level of fleas down. Steam cleaning is marvellous for carpets and upholstery; it will remove pests without harming you or your pet. But most important, if you want to minimize fleas: don't let your pets wander through the whole house and sleep on your bed!

There are three methods of coping with flies (apart from encouraging spiders—the true domestic ecologist's answer!). First, family fun with fly swats; some people are more efficient with these than others. (Confirmed ecologists will let ants tidy the remains away.) Second, hang sticky fly paper from the ceiling—but don't let your hair brush against it. Third, there's the nonchemical technofix: the electronic insect repeller used in food stores.

The Home Handyman

"Doing it yourself" around the home can create real difficulties for the PFR sufferer. There's no point in working to detoxify your system and rebuild your liver if you are being exposed to doses of chemicals that could undo all your reconstructive work in a couple of days! The sort of chemicals we use as do-it-yourselfers are very often potent liver poisons.

As with household products, the best guide to the potential danger of any substance you are using is your nose. Solvents often have a strong smell. While they will not all be equally dangerous to you, you may not know which ones to avoid until damage has occurred. It's far wiser to recognize that all of them will put a load on your detoxifying systems, and avoid them whenever you can.

This will mean that you will have to stop doing certain household jobs unless you can take the work outdoors to reduce exposure to fumes. Gluing, varnishing, wood preserving, painting (except with water-based paints), paint stripping, and cleaning brushes can be extremely hazardous in confined spaces.

Often, your body will help you to identify those chemicals that are most likely to damage you. Sensitive people tend to become highly aware of the toxicity of solvents. What you must not do is put up with them, reassuring yourself that you won't be painting this door or gluing that piece of furniture for long. The damage occurs more quickly than you realize. In molecular terms, it may not need much to trigger your liver into its dumping routine.

Even standing in fume-laden air long enough to answer the telephone can be enough to overload a chemical-sensitive system. When the floors in the house next door were painted with wood preserver, we noticed that the smell had come through to our house (although the workmen denied that they could detect it). Five minutes on our telephone, with windows and doors wide open, was enough to make me ill for two days! I had been too casual, assuming that exposure to such a low concentration of solvent for a relatively short time would not affect me.

So when you want to do these jobs, choose technology that does not involve solvents whenever you can. Remove paint with sandpaper, rather than paint stripper. Use screws instead of glue, or get someone else (preferably male) to do your gluing jobs for you. And if one of your rooms gets contaminated—stay out of it while it's thoroughly aired. Make sure you keep out until it smells safe.

Your body may tell you in other ways that something you have encountered is bad for you. A sudden desire for sweet or fattening food, or hunger beyond your normal appetite for no obvious reason, are good clues. If you experience this, try to identify the stimulus and avoid it. (Dieters who are always hungry will not get these messages, another example of how harmful working against your body can be.)

Cigarette Smoking

Finally, we cannot leave the subject of the air you breathe in your home without tackling the problem of cigarette smoke. If you are a smoker, you can probably predict some of what we have to say about it, but the reasons may be new to you.

Giving up smoking is an essential part of the PFR escape plan. You may be surprised at this, because you will know that people tend to put on weight when they give up smoking. But, as you must be well aware by now, The Plan is no ordinary way of losing unwanted fat, and its principles, although entirely logical, do not fit in with many of our usual assumptions.

There are many problems with cigarettes, some of which we describe later in this book. At this point, the important fact is that nicotine is a potent liver poison. In some ways, its effect on the liver is similar to that of DDT—nicotine can actually be used as an insecticide.

There is no way around it: you need to give up. Give up completely. You probably wish you could, just like that, and that there were no unpleasant consequences. We know the consequences. We are both ex-smokers. We know what it's like to go through withdrawal—and we know it's not the same for everybody. Perhaps for you it's particularly difficult. Or maybe you haven't been sufficiently convinced of the need to go through with it before.

So how do you give up? There are books that will help, and fact packs from the American Cancer Society, Action on Smoking and Health, and the American Heart Association. There may be an anti-smoking clinic in your area. Acupuncture helps some people.

First acknowledge that nicotine is a tranquilizer, and that's why you use it. The strategy we describe in the next chapter will help to reduce your stress level and reduce your desire for nicotine.

Choose a time to give up cigarettes when you do not expect to be under pressure. Set yourself a date and psych yourself up. Tell yourself, and your friends, colleagues, and family, that you will not smoke another cigarette after the date you've chosen. And they are not to do anything that might shake your resolve. Maybe some will join you—it's easier to give up in company with others.

Perhaps you ought to get angry about being a drug addict— angry with yourself, and angry with those commercial and political interests that want to keep you hooked. Accept that you are likely to feel anxious, miserable, sick. Withdrawal from addictive tranquilizers is almost always unpleasant. But you can do it if you want. You really can.

Avoiding Chemicals at Work

Some individual cases illustrate common problems.

Jane was a laboratory technician. She gave up her job after she realized that her blackouts, nausea, and depression were associated with exposure to the fume-laden air of her work environment.

Anna works in a modern, air-conditioned office. Everything seems very clean and efficient—but Anna has noticed that she always seems to feel sick, with headaches and a congested nose, when she's in the office. Most of her colleagues have similar experiences, although the severity of the problem varies.

Judith is a highly trained nurse. She used to work in the hospital operating room, handing the instruments to the surgeons, sometimes finishing stitching after surgery. But frequent headaches, nausea, and dizziness forced her to return to the wards.

These women are typical of thousands who work in places where the air is contaminated with chemicals that overload their detoxifying systems. Some of the most modern office buildings are known to make so many of their employees ill that a "sick building syndrome" has been identified. It is caused by the recirculation of polluted air within these buildings.

When office workers could open windows and get plenty of fresh air to breathe, the main problem was keeping warm enough. Today buildings are heated in winter and air-conditioned in summer to maintain comfortable temperatures all the year round. But, to keep the costs from becoming prohibitive, opportunities for letting in fresh air, winter or summer, are severely restricted. Under these circumstances, fumes can accumulate in the recycled air.

Sources of fumes in the modern office may not be obvious, but to the sensitive person they can pose a real threat. Old-fashioned photocopiers, carbonless copying paper, solvents used to clean equipment such as typewriters or the disk drives of computers—all these produce fumes. Add optional extras like nail-polish remover, "air freshener," and hairspray, and you can end up with a formidable chemical problem.

Places like laboratories and hospitals are very hazardous for anyone whose detoxifying capacity is limited. Solvents used for preserving and staining, antiseptic chemicals, and anesthetics all put a load on the liver. Indeed, some anesthetists and surgical nurses have developed serious liver disease from frequent exposure to small quantities of these gases.

If you are exposed to chemicals at work, you will be faced with a very tough decision. Perhaps you love nursing, or you find your job in a chemically polluted, air-conditioned office very stimulating or lucrative. You need to decide how seriously the chemical pollution of your workplace threatens you—and how important it is to you to lose that persistent fat. It may be very difficult to deal with your fat problem while you keep that job.

It is often possible to reach a compromise. Like Anna, you may be able to move away from the worst problems, while staying in the same line of work. Or you may be able to move into an office with a window that you can open. Possibly you will be able to insist on improvements in your workplace, which can reduce the chemical load—more efficient ventilation is the obvious step.

Some trade unions are very concerned about chemical hazards in the workplace and will represent your case, and those of others like you, to the management. It could well be worthwhile talking about it.

All of this may seem to present an impossibly large task. Do not be discouraged. Remember that you are searching for the particular things that adversely affect you. Because there are so many possibilities and such variation between people, it is impossible for us to say "avoid this, or that, and you will be OK." We just can't tell what is causing your problem, so we have to give very broad guidance.

Take a patient, long-term view. Listen to your body and your instincts; as you lower your general loading of pollution, you will become more sensitive to particular things. Clearing away some of the load will cause the culprits to emerge. When this happens, follow your hunches—have confidence in yourself.

Of course it would be wonderful if the world were a clean and natural place, fit for humans to live in without these problems. Changes are happening, but they take time. You can help—indeed you already are helping. By eating good, pure food, and by cleaning up your personal world, you are helping to make it better for all of us. Keep up the good work—you have nothing to lose but that unwanted fat!

12

Your Metabolism

This chapter cover stages two and three of The Plan. Stage Two has two phases, *recovery* and *warming up;* these must be completed before you begin Stage Three, *revving up* to final mobilization of remaining fat. You should not attempt to follow the later recommendations in this chapter until you have established the eating pattern described in Chapter 10 (Schedule I) and significantly reduced your environmental toxin-loading as described in the last chapter; otherwise your PFR problem could become much worse.

Remember that this is an integrated plan; all parts of it are important and must be carried out in the correct order. Check the week-by-week Action Plans (Chapter 13) if you are in any doubt.

The first objective, *recovery,* is fairly straightforward, but for many people its requirements can be all too elusive. It involves the equivalent of convalescence: eating well and getting adequate rest so that the natural recuperative powers of the body can operate.

The second, *warming up,* requires the addition of a pattern of foundation activity to adequate rest and recuperation. This will prepare you for the final part of The Plan; by this stage you will be noticing many positive benefits, including the loss of some of your fat.

You then go on to Stage Three, the final part of The Plan, where you will be *revving up* to mobilize your persistent fat. This will begin when you have sufficient detoxifying capacity to deal with the toxins you could not cope with before. This involves eating and activity patterns that will enhance your liver function in a safe and natural way. The establishment of this life-style is the final stage in getting rid of persistent fat—and keeping it off!

RECOVERY

Rest is essential for recovery and regeneration. When you are asleep, your body switches off its activity functions and concentrates instead on repairing daytime wear and tear, rebuilding long-term damage, and restructuring to meet future needs.

What you must do is ensure that you are getting enough rest. It is essential that you get a good night's sleep every night. If anything is preventing you from achieving this, you must regard it as a major problem and solve it.

If it is a matter of bad habits, you can easily change them. Too much coffee or overstimulation before going to bed are common problems. Change your routine; begin winding down earlier. Close down the stimulation or demands that are making you restless. Relaxing music, a book at bedtime, sex, a hot bath, or a short stroll may help get you into a state where you can sleep deeply and well.

If your problem is made worse by light, noise, or other people, take action against them. Turn it off, shut it out, or make them go away. Invest in comfortable earplugs, heavy lined curtains, or soundproofing. The improvement, both in your environment and in you, could be tremendous.

It may be that the way your life is structured means that such simple changes are not enough. If your routine is geared to serving the needs of others—up early to get husband or children off in the morning, the housework or job-filled day, and care, comfort, and companionship in the evenings—you have got to change it. The answer is to be selfish.

Look very carefully at where your time and effort are going. Is it really essential that you do so much for others? Is this more unwanted psychological baggage? Women can easily slip into habits of living their lives for and through others. Part of your escape from PFR is to get in control of your body; to do this you must establish some control over your life. Change the terms of your relationships with those around you; tell them why you are doing it and enlist their help. Your objective is to get time on your side so that you can rest and recuperate.

It is crucial that you minimize any factors that may be putting you under stress. This is because our whole reaction to stress is the very opposite of what we are trying to achieve with adequate rest and recuperation. Chronic stress is so destructive that it actually induces serious illness, such as heart disease and ulcers. So it is important to resolve any problems that are generating stress in your life, particularly if you know that they cause a state of chronic stress.

The general key to stress management is to reduce causes and build up your ability to cope. The later parts of The Plan will do this as an added bonus, but for now you may have to pause and concentrate on reduction. There are many books that can help. You may want to consult your doctor (do not take drugs, either for stress or to help with sleep), or perhaps specialist counseling is your answer if your relationship is generating stress.

It may be that some of your wind-down time could be spent removing stress. Many people find that specialized relaxation techniques, such as meditation or yoga, are very helpful. If these appeal to you, now is the time to follow up your interest. It is usually best to get proper instruction; find a teacher or join a class, and get expert training in the method you choose.

You can start to prime your system once you have established a routine that copes with stress and ensures that you are getting enough sleep—and that means as much as you need. Ignore other people's standards! Wake up feeling rested and have a nap in the day when you can, if you feel like it. This will aid recuperation and get you ready to mobilize that fat.

Your liver needs as much oxygen as it can get for detoxification and regeneration. You may think that because breathing is automatic, you will get as much as you need without making any special effort, but this is often not so. If you decide on yoga or meditation, controlled breathing that adds to your oxygen uptake could be a valuable part of your routine. This is another reason why we emphasized giving up smoking in the previous chapter. Not only is it very direct, personal pollution, but it reduces your oxygen-carrying capacity. When you smoke, you inhale the nicotine that keeps you hooked, and also carbon monoxide. This combines with the pigment in the red corpuscles in your blood, the hemoglobin, to form carboxyhemoglobin, which is resistant to breakdown. Thus the carbon monoxide prevents the hemoglobin from doing what it should—carrying oxygen from your lungs. Cigarette smokers can reduce their oxygen-carrying capacity by up to 20 percent in this way.

So, once more, if you are a smoker—give it up!

Even if you are not a smoker, years of tension, bad posture, or a sedentary life-style cause many people to adopt breathing patterns that do not bring as much oxygen as they need into their system. If you ever feel breathless, or have panic attacks, this could be the cause. Again, yoga breathing exercises may help.

Everyone should follow a simple breathing routine at least three times a day, to help oxygenate the body. Below is a routine that can be followed anywhere. Once a day, before you start a breathing session, check your posture. This is important simply to get your rib cage into the right shape, take restrictive pressure off your lungs, and let the whole breathing system work properly.

Use this routine to get your posture right and open up your lungs. Stand as tall as you can, with your back against a wall or other flat surface. Try to get your heels, calves, and buttocks against the wall, then as you breathe in, push your shoulders back and stretch your head up as tall as you can. Breathe in and out three times very slowly and deeply, pushing your shoulders back and head up each time. You may feel a little faint, or your heart may knock. Don't worry, it's just the unaccustomed oxygen and the pressure you have taken off your heart. Try to keep that shoulders-back, head-up posture. Think how good it is for your heart.

Once your posture is established in this position, move on to the full breathing routine. This can be done sitting, preferably on a firm chair, or lying on the floor. With your back in the new posture, think carefully about what you are doing, and breathe in very slowly, as slowly as you can. As your lungs fill and your ribs rise, think about what is happening inside; relate the feeling to the reality. When your lungs are full, try to squeeze in a little more, pushing your belly out to lower your diaphragm. When you are full, hold it as long as you can, then reverse the process, relaxing your diaphragm, then your rib cage, and empty your lungs. Hold the empty position as long as you can, then repeat. Do it at least ten times—more if you want a meditative high that is entirely natural!

At first it may be difficult to time your effort through a whole breathing cycle. Practice will get it right. And it will be quite hard work, but you will feel the supercharging effects fairly quickly. Do it any time you want to calm down or prime yourself to accomplish a difficult task.

Recovery Phase Objectives

Establish a routine that gives you plenty of sleep, ensures you can rest when necessary, and prevents you from living under continual stress.

Then build in your regular breathing routine every day.

You can link the parts together to suit yourself so that they complement each other. A positive pattern will start to emerge.

WARMING UP

While maintaining your established rest and breathing routines, the time has now come to build some activity into your life. Keep your diet patterned on that given in Schedule I, Chapter 10, and if you want to eat more as your activity level increases, do so. Trust your body; eat when you are hungry. You need plenty of good food, both for continuing recuperation and for the activity you are going to be doing.

This activity is a foundation. It is a basic minimum intended to get your systems turning over, something like breaking in a car before you start to really use it. Take your time through this stage—keep those rest and breathing patterns going!

Do not worry if you are not very physical at present. Most people who have had PFR for years will be out of condition. Just start from where you are. You will rapidly improve as all the parts of The Plan start to affect your condition. If you really need help for the absolute beginner, read "Basic Movement" or "Dance" (Appendix 4). These are basic enough to get anyone started.

While we are discussing getting started, let's deal with common blocks. Unwanted psychological baggage in this area are thoughts such as "I can't do that sort of thing," "I will feel silly," and so on. Forget it; everyone is capable of moving and becoming slim and fit. For some it will be a longer journey than for others. Even if you have never thought it possible, one step at a time will get you there. Just make up your mind to take the first step. Remember, the end of the journey is a permanently thinner you.

Enjoy yourself! When you start being active on The Plan, whatever you do, make it fun. If you are miserable, you are fighting your body again. At times it will be hard, but it should still be enjoyable. We will suggest ways that will help.

Get the right clothes. If you are a beginner, do not try to manage without the right clothes. Basics everyone should have are: a pair of good athletic shoes—the kind used by runners—with solid but padded soles, and suitable clothing, which should be minimal. Wear just enough to keep you warm. Running shorts and a tank top are great, but anything light and loose that allows movement without distraction is fine. You may also need a specialized sports bra. Remove other sources of distraction. Take off jewelry, and do not worry about hair or makeup. Time for all that later; when you are being active, be single-minded and be yourself.

Good, comfortable, and well-fitting footwear is essential, particularly if your feet are carrying a heavy load or have been distorted by too many years in high heels. Go to a specialist sports shop. No matter how "unsporty" you are now, you are moving in that direction, so start off as you mean to continue. Do not make the mistake of sliding into the department store out of embarrassment or for the pretty colors. That is fashion sportswear. It is for phonies who are not serious. Do not be shy—sports shops are usually staffed by enthusiasts, who will want to help and encourage you. And if you have never had a pair of good athletic shoes before, you will have a pleasant surprise. We know a seventy-year-old couple (now doing ten-mile sponsored walks) who said it was like having new feet!

A word of caution: if at any time after an activity session, you experience feelings of "hangover" or nausea, it means you have done too much. Wait two or three days, then try again. This time do about half as much as before. If this is OK, build up gradually; even if you feel physically capable of more, your metabolism may not be up to it yet. Patience!

In this second phase, activity is essential to bring your systems up to par. In a real sense it is the continuation of the rest and recuperation regimen described above. It is not for removing fat, although that may happen incidentally. The aim is not strenuous activity, strain, stiffness, or sweat, just a gentle buildup. Then you will be in a position to start on the last lap—shedding that TAT permanently!

What you should aim to achieve is this: a period of brisk walking for about half an hour, covering a minimum of two miles, each day. This means continuous walking, not stopping. You should be doing it every day for at least two weeks with no problems before you consider moving on to the next stage.

For some people that will be easy; others will find it a long way off. Whatever your ability, the old familiar question of having the time is most likely to be the first barrier. Take it, or make it! You are approaching the point where you can say good-bye to that weight. Don't fall back now.

If you are so overweight or out of condition that this is not possible, do not despair. The activities in Appendix 4 will start you off; when you combine them with other parts of The Plan and the increased energy output in your daily routine, you will soon be there. Take your time, and keep the rest of The Plan going.

For everyone else, time to get your athletic shoes on. Add some suitable and comfortable clothes and set off. Do not worry if you cannot walk far at first, do what you comfortably can. Remember brisk minutes are better than sloppy hours, so sing a bouncy tune in your head and stride off. Breathe deeply as you go, shoulders back, loose but purposeful. Aim for steady coordinated rhythm, swing your arms, and keep the momentum up so that it carries you along.

Measure your time at first. When you can walk continuously for thirty minutes, measure the distance you can cover, either with a map or with a car odometer. Check out some other routes, while you are about it, so you can vary your scenery.

When you come back, even if you are only out for minutes, give yourself a reward. Athletes and sportspersons have a whole wind-down routine, with a shower or bath and relaxation period. Why not you? It does not have to be anything in particular, just something you like that gives you pleasure—a little self-spoiling will encourage your efforts.

Once you have your routine established and are on the way to achieving two miles in half an hour or less, you might like to vary your activity. How about half an hour on a bike? You go a lot farther, but the breathing and the rhythmic movement are what you should aim for. Pedal briskly in a fairly low gear so that your body warms up. Or go swimming, but watch out for adverse effects from chlorinated water—stinging eyes, aching ears, skin rashes, and headaches are reported by those affected.

Now you can start to be more adventurous, perhaps with regular, energetic dancing. You are on the way to being thin and healthy, so you might as well start practicing the sort of habits that go with a thin and healthy life-style! Throughout all your activity, listen to your body, keep feeling the air flowing in and out, try to sense in your mind exactly how your muscles are moving, locate their control circuits and play with them, tense and contract, make your limbs move the way you want them to. Stretch and contract, feel the range you are capable of. Enjoy all the sensations of being in control!

How long do you need to maintain this foundation activity? What you are actually doing is rebuilding yourself, getting your body, your habits, and your attitudes back into order, so carry on as long as you are enjoying it. If you are getting restless, think about whether you are ready for the next stage, but it is important that you don't start until you are absolutely ready. False starts are very unnerving.

It takes as long as it takes, but some rough guide can be

given. The crucial thing is the state of your liver. For those under thirty who were not terribly overweight or inactive, three to six weeks should be reasonable. For those between thirty and fifty in the same condition, say four to eight weeks. Those older, or with more ground to make up, may take a lot longer. Can you carry out your half hour of activity every day without any signs of distress?

The best indication that you are ready to move on is a stable feeling of increased general health, increased energy, and clear-headedness. Watch out for false positives caused by hormone shifts in the female monthly cycle. By now you will know yourself a lot better than when you started on The Plan, and you are your best guide. If you feel ready, and vibrantly confident, then go!

REVVING UP

This is where you begin the final stage of The Plan. You should be sure that, while changing your diet and eating habits to conform to Schedule II, in Chapter 10, you maintain the low level of environmental toxins you are exposed to, and that you have got everything possible out of *recovery* and *warming up.*

At this point we must sound another warning: if you are pregnant or breastfeeding, the final stage is not yet for you. Stay with *warming up,* but take longer walks as you get healthier. Start on the final phase when your baby is weaned.

As you move into Stage Three, you should start changing your eating pattern to Schedule II, in Chapter 10. Change your eating routine gradually as you start activities that will mobilize your rebuilt liver and finally rid your body of the toxins that are locking that fat in place.

A changed pattern of physical activity is essential, because it is the only way to persuade the liver to mobilize those fat stores. Briefly, what we have to do is this: three hours after the last meal of the day, undertake enough activity to run down the liver's glycogen stores; then go to bed. While you sleep your liver will recharge—not from food, but from your fat. It's as simple as that.

It is important to realize that as you persuade your system to lose its final deposits of TAT, two things may happen. First, your body may lose other fat in preference to TAT, and second, it may still try to replace fat. Both are indications that the toxins locked up are presenting problems.

You should be prepared to allow your body to make some more fat. Your system may be using it to dilute the toxins already stored; when they are at an acceptable level it will metabolize them. So for this first stretch of the last lap, make sure those meals are big enough! Your body is adding another task to its recuperative and activity loading: it now has to actively detoxify itself. Hunger means your body is telling you it has a problem dealing with the fat you are trying to mobilize, and you should not try to override it. This doesn't mean you should stuff yourself with food when you're sure you don't want it, though!

In addition to the problem of releasing and metabolizing toxins, you will also have to be alert to other transitory problems that may occupy your liver capacity. Minor infections or other illnesses may cause reduced energy or exhaustion. If this happens, ease off; don't further overload the system. When you have recovered from the infection, press ahead again.

Warning: if the level and pattern of activity you are now embarking on produces any "hangover" effects, you must reduce your activity level. If they persist, you must go back to the previous stage. You are not ready for the last lap, and if you go on, you risk the possibility of serious damage to other organs. You cannot solve the PFR problem yet because your metabolism is clearly not yet able to cope.

You have become accustomed to a gentle, daily activity routine; now you need to speed it up. It is time to get a good warm-up suit. In summer you need shorts and a light top, or a light warm-up suit; in winter you will need a heavy, warmer suit.

This is the pattern of activity you need to follow:

Three times a week, with a gap of at least one day in between—say Monday, Wednesday, and Friday—you should spend thirty to forty-five minutes on strenuous activity, which will cause your liver to burn up its glycogen stores.

Glycogen is used up under the influence of adrenalin, so the activity needs to be violent enough to get your heart rate up, make you sweat, and keep you on the edge of breathlessness. Sound like fun? During your period of strenuous activity, you should not ease off enough to stop sweating—just enough to get your breath back, when necessary, to allow you to continue.

The body stores energy at many levels. Most of our ordinary activity just uses local energy stored in the muscles. In order to persuade your liver that you are serious, and need it to start discharging its glycogen, you have to use up these local stores. "Second wind" is the phenomenon of feeling exhausted, and then suddenly discovering new energy. The exhaustion is when the local energy is all gone, and the renewed energy is when the liver does its stuff.

Once you have completed this activity, wind down, bathe, relax, drink some water or diluted fruit juice, and go straight to bed. Remember that strenuous exercise should be done at least three hours after your last meal of the day. On the days you are not doing this, continue your breathing and relaxation. Your metabolism will still be working away for you—if you pushed it hard enough to use up that glycogen.

Don't be alarmed at the violent effects of such physical activity. Many of the things we do for fun produce these effects! Dancing, running, brisk mountain walking, weight training, hard cycling, and rowing, all produce this reaction and all are suitable. So are some traditional activities, like sawing logs, heavy digging, lawn mowing without a power-mower—a lot of things we used to do in the days before PFR was a problem for so many people.

You can use aerobic exercise, or dance exercise routines, to achieve the same effect. Whatever you do, it must be something you can work at continuously for at least half an hour. Stop-start sports like squash are not suitable. Your liver will only turn on through continuous demand—this is why athletes involved in such sports warm up first, to turn their liver glycogen on so that the energy is instantly available.

There is one possible problem you must be aware of: the activity plateau. As you push yourself, your capacity will increase—it will seem easier. It is easy to get into a routine where you do the same amount each time, but as your capacity has increased, this becomes a smaller percentage of what you are capable of, or what you need to do. You will have settled onto a stable plateau. One way to avoid this is to vary your activity; go running on Mondays, cycling on Wednesdays, and dancing on Fridays. Don't let yourself settle into a dull routine.

The rate at which you use energy during activity will be rather low at first. It will build up as your liver gets used to the idea and builds more capacity. This is the wonderful thing about physical activity: the more you do, the more you can do. One day you will look at yourself and wonder where that feeble, flabby person has gone. The new you will be a source of wonder, pleasure, and pride. When you feel that, you are on the home stretch. PFR will be a thing of the past, as will everything that goes with it.

Running is one of the best activities we know for tuning up the liver. But you should not start running before you can walk efficiently! Your Stage Two foundation should have got you to the point where you are ready; check your performance with this simple test. It will tell you whether you are ready to start running. Note your starting time, then walk two miles on level ground as briskly as you can. Do not stop. How long did it take you?

If you took more than thirty minutes, you need to do more fast walking. Similarly, if you had to stop because of leg pain, you need more practice. You are not ready for Stage Three yet! Continue walking every day; increase the speed you go and the distance you cover.

If you took between twenty-five and thirty minutes, start doing some yards of trotting every few minutes during your walk. Gradually build up the speed and distance you are trotting.

If you took less than twenty-five minutes, you are ready to start running. Warm up with an exercise routine such as the Canadian Air Force system (see References, page 210), and then go out and run. Nonrunners should start reading about technique, or ask runner friends for help; many people, especially women, simply don't know how to run, and until they learn the right type of movement, they're not likely to enjoy it. And as you are well on the way to being a physically competent, athletic person, take some time off and watch the pros on TV; see how they move. Look particularly at people whose build is like yours.

If you prefer, watch dancers or other performers. You can learn a lot by observing the way they move.

Choose the route you plan to run along with an eye to the pollution levels you'll encounter! Avoid all busy roads, and keep to paths and parks as much as you can. When you're breathing in all the air you need to keep on running, you don't want to be taking in great quantities of exhaust fumes. The same goes for cycling routes.

Throughout your activity, control your breathing; this is particularly important when running. Breathe as slowly as you can, using the control you have learned earlier. Fast panting won't deliver as much oxygen as long slow breaths. Try counting as you stride—in, two, three, out, two, three. It should come together as an integrated whole, your breathing, striding, and heart rate. This stable expression of energy over a period of time is stamina.

Push off from your toes, reach forward with your leg, and land on your heel. The foot rolls with each step. Aim for an easy, economical movement, stretch your legs, and vary your length of stride as you go.

Never push yourself too hard or too long. If you feel any pain anywhere (apart from the ache of tired leg muscles), take a rest. Don't struggle through any pain barriers. That way people injure themselves and put themselves off running—it's totally counterproductive and very, very foolish. You must not be a martyr to your exercise routine.

Do not neglect to reward yourself when you get back. A hot bath or shower will be essential now. How about a luxurious massage afterwards—your partner should oblige as a contribution toward your efforts. Keep thinking of special treats to reward yourself. There will come a time when what you are doing is its own reward. If this happens, you are hooked. You are now a confirmed physical animal and will just enjoy being physical!

For those who do not want to run, there are alternatives. Hard cycling can have excellent effects, as can dancing (leaping and throwing yourself about energetically—remember Mick Jagger?—none of that foot shuffling that could exhaust nobody); you can do it at home to your favorite records. Aerobics and "dancercise" can be good; games like tennis and soccer are fine, but only if you're an energetic player, playing hard, fast, and continuously.

When you are doing any form of strenuous activity, you will notice the signs of increased liver activity. After a few minutes of muscular work, you'll start to feel warm and you'll peel off a couple of layers of clothing. That's the first sign—the liver controls your body temperature, and it's adjusting to changing conditions. If you carry on, you'll start feeling tired; but when you experience your second wind, you'll find you can go on much further than it seemed at the start. That's the sign of the next increment in liver activity, injecting sugar into your bloodstream from its glycogen stores.

Sometimes you'll experience a less pleasant sign: pain, rather like a stitch, on the right-hand side of your body. Unlike a classic stitch, this occurs when you haven't had a meal for three hours or more before your activity began. If you slow down, rest a bit, and then continue, the pain disappears, and you find you have more energy. That may be the liver injecting nutrients into your bloodstream.

Make sure you get enough rest and recuperate sufficiently after each session of demanding activity: it is essential that you maintain yourself in excellent health so that your detoxifying capacity continues to grow.

Keep up this routine and your fat will gradually disappear. Remember to avoid the hangover zone of overactivity, but every once in a while do a little more than usual to see if you still have toxins in your system.

You may want to do less strenuous activities on alternate days. Be guided by the signals from your body; if you are sure you can cope with walking, cycling, or other activities on the days between your strenuous workouts, then go ahead. It will help to keep your systems loose and speed up the loss of fat.

What about your weight? Throughout The Plan you have been replacing unhealthy tissue with uncontaminated fat and healthy muscle, and on the last lap, you have been reducing the fat content. Your body should now have less fat and a lot of healthy tissue. You may actually be heavier, but—back to your mirror—isn't your shape much better?

You are also in control of your body; you have learned a new way of eating as much healthy food as you need, and how to protect yourself against potential hazards in your environment. You are now in a position to decide what sort of body shape you would like for the rest of your life. Chapter 13 tells you how to get and keep it.

To start on The Plan to lose your PFR you will find all the recommendations of diet, detoxification, and mobilizing your metabolism brought together in week-by-week action summaries in the following chapter. Once you have digested the information in the last three chapters and noted the sections that you feel are particularly relevant to you, you will be able to use the charts as a practical action guide.

13

Week-by-Week Action Plans

This chapter is for guidance. You must adapt the time scale to suit your personal needs, not stick rigidly to our suggestions, because they were designed for the hypothetical "average reader," and you won't be that person—she doesn't actually exist. Base your personal plan on our time scale, taking particular notice of the sequence of actions, and missing no steps on the way. Monitor your own progress and give yourself more time if you need it.

The three stages of the escape plan overlap. You will be initiating actions appropriate to one stage while continuing actions from previous stages; the beginning of a new stage does not necessarily mean the end of the last.

Throughout the early weeks it is important that you keep looking at yourself, and that you keep your self-esteem up. Remember what you are working toward, and try to think and behave like the kind of person you are going to be.

Your escape from PFR should be seen as a joyful and rewarding journey into a new way of life. There will be adventures and difficulties along the way; but it should be seen from the start as an experience you will enjoy.

WEEK 1: PREPARATORY

Your major tasks for the first week are to identify the sources of potential toxins that you encounter in your everyday life, and to prepare yourself for the changes that lie ahead.

Start keeping a detailed diary. This will add to the notes you have been making of things particularly relevant to you from the last three chapters, but it should now contain information about everything you eat, do, and feel. You should continue recording changes and events in your life as you work through the escape plan. Look back through your diary at intervals. This will contribute to your improved understanding of yourself and your progress.

Diet

Record the food you eat each day, including any snacks. Record the quantities you eat, and note how many of your food sources could cause pollution problems. Note which foods and drinks you think you could not give up easily—you could be addicted to these. How often do you normally consume them? Are you indulging at regular intervals? If so, these may be contributing to your PFR problem.

Rest

Note how much total rest you get. How much of your relaxation time is spent alone? Are you able to relax deeply when you've stopped working? How many hours are you sleeping? Can you identify anything that interferes with your sleep?

Note when you feel tired or sleepy. Is sleepiness associated with eating meals or particular foods? It could be a sign of sensitivity. Are you able to rest when you feel tired?

Activity

How far do you walk (or bicycle) each day? How often do you use the car? Do you drive when there's no real need to? If you habitually wear high-heeled shoes or clothes that limit your activity, start changing to styles that give greater comfort and freedom of movement.

Environmental Pollution

Go through the questionnaire (p. 109) to determine the pollution level in your home. Start discarding air pollutants such as insecticides, "air fresheners," and sprays.

Smokers: record the number of cigarettes you smoke, and when you smoke them. What are the circumstances that induce smoking?

If you work away from home, check potential sources of pollution in your work environment. Record all you find.

Psych-Up

Use a full-length mirror to acknowledge what you are. Assert your own importance and take action against rejection of yourself. Look at yourself with appreciation.

Throw away the bathroom scales and persuade yourself to forget about your weight.

Action

Find organic food suppliers and health-food cookbooks. Start sprouting mung beans.

Use the first step of the breathing routine (p. 125) to improve your posture and breathing habits. Make a point of always standing tall and proud.

Appraisal

At the end of the week, look at the information you've gathered about yourself. You're gaining insight into the nature of your personal problem—and that's a big step toward solving it.

WEEK 2: STAGE ONE. DETOXIFICATION

During the second week, you will be concentrating on removing sources of potential toxins. At the same time, you should prepare yourself for Stage Two.

Diet

Stock up with basic supplies of YES foods, and phase out processed foods. Sprout beans and grains. Experiment with ways of preparing food that will fit in with your PFR diet.

Rest

Establish a Positive Rest Routine. Deal with problems that stop you from getting as much rest or sleep as you want: make this a priority. Try building naps into your day if possible—perhaps in the afternoon or midevening. Give up coffee and other stimulants.

If your relaxation problems are associated with stress, plan to deal with the major causes. Find help (counselors, yoga teachers, support groups) if appropriate. Give yourself plenty of time to solve these problems—but start working on them now.

Breathing

Start a full deep-breathing cycle (see p. 125). Practice each night before bed.

Medication

Medication users should find out about alternative methods of dealing with their problems. Discuss phasing out your drugs with your doctor. The comments on stress, above, may be relevant. Your life-style changes in future weeks will help.

Users of the "Pill" should explore barrier methods of contraception (diaphragm, sheath) or the possibility of sterilization.

Activity

Buy some good athletic shoes and start breaking them in.

Environmental Pollution

List the hazards you're going to eliminate first. Work out how to manage without them, and acquire substitutes if necessary. Work through your list, crossing them off one by one.

Smokers, start planning when you'll give up. Investigate stress-reduction methods if you think you'll need them.

Identify hazards at work, and seek ways to reduce them.

WEEK 3: STAGE ONE CONTINUES, STAGE TWO. RECOVERY BEGINS

During Week 3, action on environmental pollution and dietary change continues. Stage Two work includes breathing exercises and basic activity.

Diet

Get established on the PFR diet (Schedule I). Continue sprouting beans, seeds, etc. What else can you grow yourself? Check out organic gardening books and seed displays in garden shops if you haven't grown your own before. If you believe you're allergic to some of the YES foods, start the diet without them, but always make sure that you're eating comparable foods in equivalent quantities. For example, you may want to substitute rice and millet for wheat, or nuts and seeds for eggs.

Note any withdrawal symptoms you experience with your changed diet. You could be allergic to the foods or drinks you most crave. Don't give in—give it time. You will feel much better after a week.

Rest

Continue to make sure that you get plenty of sleep.

Breathing

Practice deep-breathing exercises three times daily.

Activity

Start building up your stamina with frequent walks. If you are unaccustomed to physical activity, try the "Dance" advice in Appendix 4.

Environmental Pollution

Initiate action to reduce pollution at work if necessary. Finish removing hazards from your home.

WEEK 4: STAGE TWO, RECOVERY CONTINUES, STAGE TWO. WARMING UP BEGINS

By the fourth week you should be established on the Schedule I diet. Rest and breathing exercises remain important. Daily activity initiates Stage Two of The Plan.

Diet—Schedule I

Five small meals a day, drawn from the YES group of foods. Give up tea, coffee, and alcohol completely; substitute mineral water, diluted fruit juices, vegetable juices, herb teas, Postum, and/or dandelion coffee.

Make sure you have sufficient sprouts for each day—vary the seeds, beans, etc. Try different types, such as alfalfa, wheat, and sunflower.

Eat some raw cashew nuts, brazil nuts, and/or sunflower seeds daily.

Women may wish to add evening-primrose oil as a dietary supplement—especially during the second half of the monthly cycle. Vitamin B6 may also be helpful for those who have premenstrual problems that might cause yearnings for chocolate, etc.

Rest

Remember you're still treating yourself as a convalescent. Get as much rest as you need to maximize healing.

Breathing

Do breathing exercises three times daily.

Activity

Walk or bicycle for half an hour each day.

WEEKS 5 TO 7: STAGE TWO. WARMING UP

During these weeks you will be gradually increasing the intensity of your daily activity sessions, while maintaining your rest and breathing routines. This will improve liver function.

Diet—Schedule I

If you left particular foods out of your diet because of suspected allergy, now is the time to try them out. Introduce them one at a time, no more than one per day. If you react badly to one or more of these foods, don't try it again for two months. Never eat any food to which you have shown signs of allergy more than twice weekly, and then only in small amounts. However, you may find that you are not allergic to the organically produced form of the food you thought you couldn't tolerate.

You may have been reacting to the residues in it, and may have no problems with uncontaminated forms.

Rest
You should have established a regimen that ensures that you do not feel tired when you wake in the morning, and that lets you nap during the day if necessary. If this is proving difficult, find a yoga or meditation teacher, or learn a technique for deep relaxation.

Breathing
Continue deep-breathing exercises regularly.

Activity
Gradually increase the length of your daily walks. Make sure you are walking briskly, with a good, upright posture that allows slow, deep breathing. Focus on your muscles as you move. Find new routes in your neighborhood, explore local parks and woods. Take a longer walk once or twice a week, or go swimming or dancing to vary your activity routine.

Environmental Pollution
Have you given up smoking yet? If not, do it now. Help the other members of your household to give up if they are polluting the air you breathe.

WEEKS 8 TO 12: STAGE TWO. WARMING UP

During these weeks, your major task is to stimulate your liver so that it is capable of dealing with greater toxin loads, without dumping residues into fat.

Diet—Schedule I
You may want to increase your carbohydrate intake (roots and grains) as your activity level rises. If you feel hungry—eat!

Rest
Don't neglect it!

Breathing

Continue deep-breathing exercises; you need the oxygen.

Activity

Continue daily rhythmic activity, sufficient to make you feel very warm and increase your heart rate. Add varied activities.

Test your walking speed. Are you ready to start gentle running? Push yourself harder—but beware exercise "hangovers" and infections—don't take it too fast.

Warning

Pregnant or lactating women, elderly people, and those with health problems should not progress past this stage. Stay at this level and burn off your excess fat gradually.

Do not continue past this point until you can comfortably walk two miles on level ground in twenty-five minutes or less.

WEEKS 13 TO 18: STAGE THREE. REVVING UP

During these weeks you will be increasing your rate of metabolism, increasing your oxygen use, and beginning to mobilize fat stores.

Diet—Intermediate between Schedules I and II

The transition from five small meals per day to one main one should be gradual. Be conscious of how you feel; let the state of your body guide your actions. Boost carbohydrate intake. Eat about three meals per day of YES foods, plus snacks as required. Drink plenty of pure water, especially after activity.

Rest

This must balance your activity. Make sure you relax after every session. Sleep remains important.

Activity

Alternate days of 30 to 45 minutes of strenuous activity, three days per week. Running is strongly recommended. Make sure you do enough to finish your session thoroughly tired and bathed in sweat. Watch out for exercise "hangovers"—drop back to Stage Two if you suffer warning signs such as headaches, nausea, and general malaise associated with exercise or developing the morning after.

Never continue working a sore knee, ankle, or joint—there's no need to risk injuring yourself! Read health and sports magazines for ideas and guidance on activities.

Do just enough gentle activity on "off" days to keep loose and mobile.

If you feel tired or sick, cut back activity and increase rest. Never do strenuous exercise when you have a cold.

WEEKS 19 TO 25: STAGE THREE. MOBILIZING FAT

At this point you will be sufficiently active to burn off your excess fat at a steady rate. Your pattern of strenuous activity followed by rest and fasting will encourage the development of a larger and more efficient liver.

Diet—Schedule II
Eat one major meal each day; other meals should be much smaller. From three hours before your evening activity session until midmorning the next day, eat nothing; drink only water, diluted fruit juice, or herb tea. The exception to this rule is when your activity has been so demanding that hunger wakes you in the night; do not ignore it, get up and eat. Plain yogurt, with granola and fruit if desired, is recommended.

On nonactivity days, you can eat in the evening if you feel hungry.

Adjust food intake to match increasing energy use. Resist any temptation to force your body to shed fat quickly.

Rest
Always allow complete recuperation after activity sessions. We are building up now!

Activity
Alternate days: warm up with stretching and body-bending (Canadian Air Force exercises if you like). Follow warm-up with 30 to 40 minutes of running or similar strenuous activity. Wind

down afterward with a warm bath or shower and go to bed to relax completely.

Other days: gentle activities only, whatever feels right to you. Some bicycling, or walking if desired.

WEEKS 26 TO 40: STAGE THREE. MOBILIZING FAT CONTINUES

By this time you will be enjoying the results of your efforts, but you probably have more fat to lose. The basic pattern of the plan remains unchanged.

Diet—Schedule II
You should be able to cope with some formerly forbidden substances such as coffee and your favorite cheeses now, but keep your intake low. The YES foods should still form your staple diet.

Activity
Use your new abilities to widen your activity interests. Consider specific activities for problem muscle groups; twice-weekly sessions of weight training will build a more desirable body shape. Start to live the thin life, with habitual activity. Take a long walk or bicycle ride (two hours or more) once a week.

FROM WEEK 41 ON: MAINTENANCE

Having worked through the escape plan, you will have lost much of your persistent fat. At this stage you should choose meal times and activities to suit your own needs. Now that you know how your body reacts, you are able to make informed choices.

Diet
Eat as desired, but make sure you keep pollution levels low. Continue to select mainly from YES foods, but whether you eat according to Schedule I, Schedule II, or some other routine is up to you. In general, women should have frequent small meals,

while men should eat greater quantities less often. Don't let yourself slip into dangerous dietary habits.

Activity
To maintain a good body shape, you have to stay very active. Choose the types of activities you prefer, and those that produce the kind of body you think you could achieve. The leanest women are long-distance runners and bodybuilders—but they train for many hours each week to achieve their shapes. In general, the more physically active you are, the thinner you can expect to be.

Environmental Pollution
Campaign for a less polluted world. Join Greenpeace and other concerned bodies—add your voice to the growing chorus of protest.

14

Permanent Good Shape

When you've got yourself into good shape, you'll want to keep it for the rest of your life.

By now, having worked through The Plan, you will know yourself very well. You will have a realistic self-image, there will be no need for scales or calorie counters, and diets will be of no interest to you. You will understand how your body is working, what makes it want to put on fat, and how you can control it. You should also be a more physically competent and healthier person. We hope that, in addition to learning how much activity you need to keep your metabolism at its best, you will also enjoy being active.

You should also be a happier person. In coming to terms with PFR, you will have been forced to throw out a lot of unwanted psychological baggage: those values and beliefs that may work for the benefit of others, but against your self-interest. You will have restructured crucial areas of your life to suit your individual needs. Growing awareness of these needs should have convinced you of your value as an individual; the control you now have over your body and your life is a very positive thing. From here you can go on to further fulfillment and achievement as you wish. You have, after all, solved the problems that are major preoccupations and stumbling blocks for most people.

Not only are you well on the way to being an expert in that most important subject, yourself, but you will also be wiser about the ways of the world. You should be looking with new eyes at innovations in food and chemical products. Your suspicion of their potential effects will be based on your personal experience. The general state of the environment will also be in your mind. You may now see that, just as we cannot pollute the food we eat without harming ourselves, so we cannot pollute the world in general without causing harm.

So avoiding PFR and staying thin involves maintaining a positive life dynamic on many levels. You will have to eat wholesome food for the rest of your life—nothing wrong with that. You will have to keep your personal loading of potential toxins as low as possible. As long as you avoid the substances that prompt your system to create fat, the amount of weight you carry will be up to you.

The key to success is simple. If you want to be thin, beautiful, and energetic, you have to live the life of a thin, beautiful, and energetic person. If you live in any other way, you will become a reflection of that life-style. Before your understanding of the PFR Syndrome, this would have been a meaningless statement and an unattainable ideal. Now that you know what has been happening to you, it is quite realistic.

Having mastered PFR, some of the old rules start to make a little sense again. If you eat innocent food, excess calories will tend to be stored in fat for energy. Activity will tend to mobilize any excess fat. But you will always be at risk of PFR, and you cannot simply drop back into your old ways—that caused the problem in the first place.

Your understanding of the functions of fat on your body will allow you to see why you are carrying what you are. You can adjust your life-style, its pace and tempo, to choose how much fat you have.

In the long term, women should adjust their eating pattern to a more "female" one. They should be mainly vegetarian nibblers, eating from hour to hour whatever they need for their immediate needs. In this way, that minimal subcutaneous layer should not be activated too often, either to store energy or discharge it. Because of the smaller female liver, women's energy needs are best met on a more immediate hour-by-hour basis; unlike men, they are not designed to eat widely spaced, large meals. Men and women are different in many ways other than purely sexually; understanding this and eating accordingly will help you avoid some weight pitfalls.

There will be a delicate, and individual, balance between the amount you can eat and the size of your fat reserves. As an ex-PFR sufferer, you must ensure at all times that you eat enough food. Adjust to any surplus by increasing your daily activity levels. This is the only method that will work for you, and anyone else for that matter; if you attempt passive weight loss you are heading for trouble. Your body will start losing lean tissue again, with the possibility of tipping you back into PFR. At what point that might happen is entirely unpredictable. It depends on too many variables. So play safe, eat enough good organic food, don't go hungry, and adjust your weight by changing your activity levels.

This applies to all ages. As you grow older your metabolism tends to slow down, which means that you can manage with less food. But eating less requires extra vigilance about the quality of your food and about environmental pollutants. And, unexpectedly, it may also mean that you have to be more active to keep in shape. Ballerinas, who have to keep superfit and shapely, find that, as they pass their twenties, they have to put more and more work into keeping 100 percent in shape for their career. Realistically, we are not aiming for this extreme, but the principle behind it still operates for a lot of people.

Keeping in shape through an active life has two advantages. First, you will be a naturally healthier person; after a little while living like this, you will be amazed at how feeble those around you seem. Your liver and detoxified systems will be dealing with all those minor infections that afflict people all the time, without your noticing it; you just won't catch all those illnesses that are around. And the likelihood of your suffering major, debilitating conditions, from heart disease to cancer, will be much reduced.

Second, you can decide on the kind of body shape you want to have. Within the limits of your skeletal structure, and the effects of your hormones (which you in turn influence), you can shape your body to your personal desires—not only in general terms of thinner or more rounded, but also in specifics, more shapely legs, thinner thighs perhaps, or better shoulders. What you want is within your grasp; this is what being in control is all about!

Under that fine layer of healthy fat that gives your body its sexual shaping and smooth surface, your shape is determined by your muscles. Our social values used to lead women to believe that muscles were at best undesirable, and at worst uncouth. Since every movement, from the merest arching of an eyebrow to leaping in the air, depends on our muscles, this view was clearly unrealistic. Fortunately, attitudes are changing. Even the least athletic women now understand how important good muscles and good muscle tone are to maintain their desired condition.

It will take time and effort. There is no way around this. We evolved to be active creatures and it is only by directing that activity, by the details of the way we move and use our bodies, that we maintain a good shape. This is an essential part of the thin and healthy life-style. Now that you have lost your PFR, you are no longer misled by claims made for unhealthful, processed food; if you are tempted by claims for easy ways of keeping in shape, apply the same critical appraisal that you should to all commercial enterprises. Ask yourself, who is going to get more shapely, you or their bank balance?

Similarly, you should read magazine articles which describe the weight-loss or beauty secrets of the stars with a critical eye. What they don't tell you may be more important than what they do. Raquel Welch put it very honestly and succinctly when asked how she kept her desirable shape—"I work my butt off."

Another opening line that should arouse your suspicion is this: "The latest scientific research has discovered . . ." Often an insignificant diet or piece of gadgetry is offered as the universal answer that will allow people to disregard totally the reality of their nature and reappear magically unscathed, thin, and beautiful, if only they buy the product of this research. We notice with amusement, when reviewing this sort of thing, that the people making the extravagant claims never seem to benefit from their wares in the way that they say you will. They are, if not fat, usually looking seedy and hardly athletic. Ignore them, and those stars who may sell them testimonials; if the new panacea has only just been discovered, it can hardly have affected their lives in the way they suggest.

For muscles, as for other bodily systems, it is true that if you don't use them, you will lose them. There are two approaches to keeping in shape, and you will already be aware of the conflict of interests involved. You can live in a way that is basically bad for you and hope to compensate by adding some sport or exercise on top. Or you can live in a way that is good for you, and add, as required, specific activities or pleasurable pursuits. The Plan you have been following is a bit of a hybrid; it has to work for people with many different constraints on their lives.

In the short term, it may not matter which approach you follow. However, if you opt for, or are forced to follow, the former, you must understand that your life-style will bring diminishing returns. This may be all right for a limited period, while you are young and establishing yourself in your career, but you should put a time limit on it. It is easy to drift into living in unsatisfactory ways.

Obviously, if you could structure your life so that all your daily needs for activity were met by the way you lived, this would be ideal. Few of us are in the fortunate position of athletes or other stars. But we can, and should, take every opportunity life offers to change in that direction. It is a matter of having the right philosophy and view of your own importance.

Whichever way your life is going, you need to work those muscles. A good regimen for basic fitness and figure maintenance can be found in *Physical Fitness*, the system developed for both men and women by the Royal Canadian Air Force. It is a good daily foundation system because it only takes about a quarter of an hour for the routine—half an hour with a shower—and because the routines themselves are progressively graduated. This means that you can start at any level and progressively work up.

There is no reason at all why you should not continue with the activities you started while working through The Plan. You could follow them and also take up some sport you may have long considered. Skiing, perhaps? Energetic summer days on the tennis courts? Or both—why not? If you do take up a sport, bear in mind what the Wimbledon stars say: they don't play tennis to keep fit, they have to keep fit to play tennis. If you do take part in a particular sport, it will add to your fitness, but it will not necessarily maintain it.

For specific body contouring, the rules are fairly straightforward. If you want thin thighs or a flat stomach, shapely buttocks or a firm bosom, you have to find an exercise routine that works the muscle groups in that problem area. Once this routine has reduced the burden of unwanted bulk, you can then decide whether to add more firm shape with more muscle, or to reduce the muscle bulk, trimming it down, without replacing it with fat.

To increase bulk, you need slow movements with a high resistance and a low number of movement repetitions. Weight training is the best method; make sure you warm up completely first, and combine it with your other activities. Do not try to use weight training as a substitute for your regularly scheduled exercise routine.

If on the other hand you wish to reduce the size of a particular muscle group, you need faster movements, lower resistance, and higher numbers of repetitions. There are many specialized sources of advice of this kind of bodybuilding. It should be easy to find activity routines which, combined with your new physical competence, will achieve the desired end.

Before you turn into Superwoman, you should take a look at the context of your life. We have found that many people who start off on a campaign to improve their lives are both surprised at the degree to which they succeed, and unprepared for that success.

The main problem area is with personal relationships. If you are steaming away to become thin and athletic, and your partner stays where he is, it is quite possible that you will grow apart. You are, after all, becoming a different person. To escape PFR, you are changing your life-style and life dynamic in many ways, some subtle, some obvious, but all will have an effect. If you are married and have a family, there could be problems if you don't anticipate and plan ahead.

The ideal would be to take your partner and your kids with you into a new and better future. This will be possible if you treat PFR, and your determination to stay thin and healthy, as a shared project. They may not be PFR victims—but The Plan will improve the health and vitality of anyone. And removing the pollution from their lives may be a necessary part of removing the pollution from your own. So, if you could all work on it together as a family unit, everyone would benefit.

If you are free and single, there may not be problems of this sort. In fact, for you, escaping the PFR Syndrome and setting your life on a more positive and dynamic course is likely to be only beneficial. Nevertheless, you will be changing over a period of time, and you should be aware of the potential impact on your life.

Women should watch out for men becoming insecure. If you have transformed yourself from an unhappy blob into a lithe and competent person before his eyes, your partner may not be able to cope with the new you. Of course, at many levels he will be pleased, but at some levels he may be worried; will he be able to maintain the balance in your relationship that he was used to? It is likely that the answer is no. And this is probably another healthy result of your efforts, because there may have been some degree of complicity on his part in maintaining your previous unhappy state. But you should be able to build something more positive from your new position; you may have to take a bit more of the initiative and exercise more power within your relationships than you have been accustomed to.

In effect, you will have become a younger, more vibrant person. If you have a stable relationship, it is better if you can make these kinds of journeys together. Don't worry about the kids—they will think it's great if you are joining in more of their games and sports, instead of being one of those prematurely, metabolically senile young moms, old before their time, always watching from the sidelines. Life is for living, not watching!

For long-term health, it is important that you get yourself into a balanced way of life, a stable routine that suits you. And use your new awareness to spread the idea that health for everyone depends on a balanced relationship between us and the rest of the biosphere—the health of the person is the health of the planet. Maintaining this balance is the key to permanent good shape, to permanent good health, and to a long and enjoyable life.

15

PFR—
The Theoretical Model

In this chapter we shall consider some theoretical aspects of the PFR Syndrome. You may find some of the ideas difficult to grasp because they are unfamiliar. You do not need this knowledge to overcome your PFR problem, but we believe that it could help you to fit the escape strategy more precisely to your personal needs.

To understand the mechanism involved in PFR we have to take a look at liver functions. The liver is little short of awe-inspiring. It is a marvelous organ, the largest gland in the body and in many ways the most complicated. It carries out twenty-two known major functions, ranging from the digestion and storage of food, the synthesis of body constituents, and the regulation of the chemical balance of the blood, to temperature control.

The liver lies on the right-hand side of the body behind the ribs, just under the diaphragm. It is closely interconnected with the heart and the nervous system at many levels. It is linked to the small intestine by a special vein (the hepatic portal vein), which carries food constituents absorbed through the lining of the intestines.

The liver secretes bile, which pours out through the bile duct into the duodenum, just below the stomach. Bile plays a crucial role in fat digestion. Most of the bile is reabsorbed by the intestines and recycled by the liver, very little being lost in the process.

Blood rich in digestive products and the assortment of chemicals that we take in with our food and drink circulates through six-sided liver "lobules" where the complicated processes of biotransformation take place. Chemicals that enter are modified in a wide variety of ways by the host of enzyme systems that each cell contains.

Protein synthesis is one of the jobs done by the liver lobule cells. In the intestines, food is broken down so that proteins arrive in the liver in the form of amino acids, the building blocks of all living tissue. The enzyme systems of the liver take these amino acids and reassemble them into proteins that are useful to us. These are then secreted into an exit vein that carries them to the heart, which pumps them around the rest of the body.

Carbohydrate foodstuffs are digested so that they arrive at the liver as glucose. The liver cells then build some of this into a long-chain simple carbohydrate called glycogen. Glycogen is stored in the liver itself, from which it can be quickly mobilized to provide energy when necessary—for instance, to fuel a burst of physical activity. If you suddenly have to sprint to escape from a predator, or if you decide to do a bout of any strenuous activity, the local store of fuel in your muscles will run out very quickly. It is replenished by glycogen from the liver, which is broken back down into glucose again and released into the bloodstream under the influence of the flight-or-fight hormone, adrenalin.

In men, the liver's glycogen store is very large. It evolved under conditions of life in our distant past, when men were hunters. Women have much smaller glycogen stores in livers that are smaller both in absolute terms and in relation to their total body size. They have evolved different fueling systems to suit their prehistoric roles as gatherer and mother. Women's bodies tend to run on shallow reserves of energy and to store fuel in the more slowly released but longer-lasting form of fat, principally in that troublesome subcutaneous layer.

The liver also acts as a store for certain vitamins and minerals. It is generally known that liver can be an excellent food; this is mainly because it is so rich in the stored vitamins A, B group, and D, as well as iron and zinc.

The role of the liver in the digestion, storage, and release of nutrients into the rest of the body is the reason we described it earlier as a vast warehouse; as you will now realize, it is also the body's prime industrial area. From this power base, it regulates metabolism throughout the rest of the body. The nervous and hormone systems provide feedback loops that allow this regulation to occur. However, it is not a one-way process—the liver responds to needs, as well as directing them.

Any body product that is available for recycling will go through the liver. Every part of our body is constantly being used, broken down, and replaced. It is a part of that process of homeostasis we mentioned in Chapter 2. The products of breakdown reach the liver, where they are either sent off for excretion or reused. One example is bile pigments, which are actually made by the liver from the debris of red blood corpuscles.

This is another reason for the development of detoxifying capacity in the liver. Some products of normal metabolism are themselves toxic. Some parts of the body, such as the intestine, produce ammonia, which is poisonous in more than very small concentrations. The liver lobules change ammonia into urea, which can then be eliminated, through the kidneys, in urine.

The crucial issue in PFR is the role of the liver in the conversion of chemicals foreign to our bodies; these include substances of natural origin, but also, more especially, those artificial substances produced by man.

During evolution, which produced our sexually differentiated livers and their relatively different metabolisms working under the influence of different hormone mixtures, we encountered environmental toxins. These were toxins in plants and fungal by-products, and toxins produced by bacteria. Some of these can still occur in the human diet, especially in the tropics. The metabolic systems that our ancestors developed now have to cope with the massive chemical load to which we are exposed daily. This load consists of tens of thousands of entirely artificial substances.

The substances that end up in our bloodstream are dealt with in those liver lobule cells that are already busy handling digestion and recycling nutrients. To carry out this work, each liver cell relies on a kind of sub-cell within it, the mitochondrion. Mitochondria are sausage-shaped structures, consisting of libraries of hundreds of enzymes designed to deal with any substance the cell may encounter. There are many mitochondria in each liver cell. Each cell in the body has mitochondria; thus a molecular message sent out by the liver can be reinterpreted by reference to a similar library of enzyme information when it reaches its destination.

One enzyme system among the liver-cell mitochondria is known as Cytochrome P-450. There are, in fact, a number of Cytochrome P-450s. At first it was assumed that just one enzyme had the particular characteristics that identified this class, but, as with vitamins and many other chemical components of our incredibly complicated bodies, further research is constantly revealing more forms.

C P-450s are capable of catalyzing a range of oxidative chemical reactions. Specifically, this means they can cause a poison or drug molecule to react with oxygen, and while C P-450s must be present for this to occur, they are left unchanged at the end of the reaction. Other chemical substances, both complex organic molecules and minerals, including iron, are also involved; but, like the cytochromes, while they must be present for the reaction to occur, they are not actually used up in the process.

This is the first stage of metabolism of such substances. The rate at which it occurs depends on the availability of appropriate C P-450s and on oxygen from the air we breathe. This stage is blocked by carbon monoxide—which is present in the blood of smokers in a concentration that is directly proportional to the number of cigarettes they smoke.

Because there are many C P-450s catalyzing a range of different reactions, there can be many products of this first stage of metabolism. Each drug or toxin can in fact be altered in a lot of different ways. The problem is that the products of these reactions are often more poisonous than the original substance. This is because they have been made more chemically reactive by the addition of oxygen, and another step in metabolism must follow quickly to deal with this hazard.

The second stage of toxin metabolism usually involves a substance called glutathione. This attaches to the reactive intermediate and alters it so that it is no longer so dangerous to the body. However, glutathione is in limited supply, so sometimes this second stage of metabolism cannot keep pace with the production of highly reactive poisons by the C P-450 system. Under these circumstances, the liver—and the rest of the body—can get poisoned.

The problem of the increased reactivity of oxidized metabolic products, and their frequently dangerous nature, plus the apparently illogical shortage of glutathione, is a relic from our very distant past. It is a reminder that oxygen was a highly poisonous substance for life on this planet at one time. Most cellular components are still protected from it; they function anaerobically, that is, in the absence of oxygen. Aerobic activity occurs at a series of progressively restricted sites, from our lungs, through our bloodstream, to those actual cellular reactions that require oxygen for the release of chemical energy.

The dangers of the shortage of glutathione can be illustrated by what can happen when someone takes an overdose of the popular painkiller, acetaminophen (Tylenol). The C P-450s add oxygen to the basically fairly innocuous acetaminophen molecule—and make it into a very dangerous substance. If there is not enough glutathione available in the liver to complete the second stage of metabolism, liver damage results. Death from liver failure occurs days or even weeks after the overdose.

Obviously, the body has ways of coping with slight imbalances. In most biological reactions, the rate at which the first one or two stages of a sequence occur depends partly on the rate at which subsequent steps are occurring. There are systems of feedback that allow the processes to be self-limiting and safe. But the picture can be further complicated by the effects of certain chemical substances on the C P-450 system itself.

The effect of many products developed by the chemical industry is to interfere with the checks and balances in this crucial detoxification system. Drugs such as barbiturates, many pesticides, certain industrial chemicals, and components of cigarette smoke are capable of speeding up the C P-450s, thus causing the reactions they catalyze to occur preferentially. The technical term for this process is *induction*. The result can be a range of strange and dangerous intermediates, produced at a higher than normal rate.

Such intermediates have been linked with cancer. The ability of cigarette smoke to alter the detoxification systems of the liver in this way could account for the fact that smoking is associated with cancers in many parts of the body where the smoke itself never goes. These include cancer of the liver itself, and of the cervix, bladder, pancreas, and other organs.

One general class of compounds that are known to speed up the C P-450 system is called "polycyclic hydrocarbons." These are compounds that have two or more rings of carbon molecules in them. Artificial substances with this type of molecular structure are very common products in our industrialized culture.

We spray billions of gallons of polycyclic hydrocarbon insecticides every year, but just because we are not dying like flies or other bugs, we would be foolish to imagine we can escape without any harmful effect. The human body has a marvelous ability to resist the effects of potentially lethal chemicals, but they have to compete for the limited resources of the detoxifying enzyme systems. These systems are linked up with other biochemical processes in our bodies, and thus a further range of secondary effects may be generated.

The C P-450s are important, for example, in the metabolism of hormones. Sex hormones and steroids, both of which occur naturally and are produced in synthetic forms for therapy and convenience, are structurally related to polycyclic hydrocarbons. As such they will be broken down in the same sort of way. So altering the balance of metabolic pathways could have implications for the body's response to its own hormones.

The effects can be quite subtle. It is feasible to assume, for example, that the hormone imbalance that produces premenstrual tension could be linked with an imbalance in the enzyme systems of the liver. The metabolism of stress hormones, also, could be altered, producing exaggerated hazards from high levels of stress hormones circulating throughout the body. We consider such possibilities in more detail in the final chapter.

The questions we are raising here concern the way different organic substances interact with one another. These interactions involve both natural and artificial products, those that originate within the body and those we take in from outside. One documented area of interaction is through induction of the C P-450 system. A general consequence is likely to be a state of overload in the second stage of detoxification. Others, including competition for transport systems, are known; more undoubtedly exist, but are as yet unidentified.

PFR involves transporting unwanted and potentially dangerous substances into storage organs where they will do little damage. For organic compounds of the type we have been discussing, the store is fat. Most are readily dissolved in fat and can stay there in a reasonably stable state for as long as necessary.

Potentially dangerous chemicals are not normally allowed to float around freely in the bloodstream. They are attached to special carriers for transport from one place to another. In the liver, these carriers are known as ligandins: we think of them as biological wheelbarrows. Again, there can be competition among different metabolic products for these wheelbarrows; many can be moved by the same ligandin, but the availability may be limited—like taxis on rainy days.

Once at a suitable deposit point, in this case a fat cell, the carrier will release its toxic load into solution in the fatty interior. This is possible only if the concentration of chemicals already in solution in the fat is not too high. For the dumping system to work at its best, the body may need to add fat to the cells to increase their volume and thus reduce the concentration of toxins within.

Obviously, this protective mechanism is itself finely balanced. The liver must be working efficiently enough to make fat available to pump up the fat cells to cushion the effects of poisons. Your body must have an adequate quantity of fat cells, and the systems for filling them must function quickly and effectively. And there must be sufficient calories in the diet to allow the deposition of fat.

If these conditions are not met when the liver is overloaded or stimulated into producing poisonous metabolites of the chemicals it processes, then the effects of the poisons will be much worse. Instead of getting fat, you are likely to get sick. When the capacity of the liver to adapt and use different metabolic pathways is limited by poisons or disease, it may not be capable of dealing with chemicals in this way. In some conditions, such as cirrhosis due to alcohol, it has been observed that sufferers can be quite obese in the early stages of the disease, when the overloaded liver is shifting toxins into fat. Then, as the condition progresses and the liver becomes less and less capable of functioning normally, they start to waste away.

This, then, is how poisons can make you fat. Because of the body's need to protect itself, it will set up and give priority to this complete chain of reactions. This is the metabolic basis of the Persistent Fat Retention Syndrome.

Once the metabolism has established this mechanism, its preferential use will tend to be established. Preferentiality may produce some addictive reaction to the substances that the body treats in this way. The system comes to anticipate the overloading they provide and behaves disruptively if this anticipation is not fulfilled.

Stores of fat saturated with toxins are what we have called toxic adipose tissue—TAT. Its status is constantly monitored by the body, and especially by the central chemical control center, the liver. Fat is a relatively stable store, because it is not involved in active metabolic processes most of the time, and it does not have a plentiful blood supply, but it is nevertheless kept in equilibrium with the general chemical balance of the body. If the blood is loaded with poisons but the fat cells are relatively free of them, then more will be dumped in fat; but if the blood is clear of poisons, then they will tend to be picked up from fat to be dealt with by the liver.

If the liver successfully completes its metabolic sequence, unwanted chemicals can finally be eliminated from the body. The most used route is through the kidneys, which filter water-soluble products from the blood. Even at this stage, some of these substances may still be poisonous. While they are bound to their biological carriers in the blood, they do no damage; but when they leave them in the tubules of the kidneys, they are capable, once more, of causing injury. Many drugs and chemicals are known to poison liver and kidney alike.

We have referred so far mainly to recognized poisons, for it is the metabolism of these that has been studied by toxicologists. But what your body treats as poisonous will not be just those chemicals that are known to poison everybody. You may react to a wide range of normally harmless substances as though they were poisonous, because your body has misidentified them. This is the basis of allergy, and it can form a separate route into PFR for those susceptible.

In the context of a heavy environmental loading of artificial substances that have a high affinity with our biology, problems are bound to arise. The systems concerned will be chronically overloaded, and this is exactly what precipitates allergic responses. An allergy is a changed response to a stimulus; usually it is thought of as an exaggerated and inappropriate response to a food or other substance.

In our case histories, we outlined an example of one person, predisposed to allergic responses, who subsequently developed a cyclic PFR response to his allergic condition. The allergic route into PFR is less clear than the mechanism of detoxification overload detailed above; nevertheless, some features can be sketched in.

Allergic reactions of all sorts are increasing. The classic condition, hayfever, now affects between 10 and 15 percent of the population in every industrialized nation. Hayfever was unknown two hundred years ago. The first recorded victims were doctors, who had difficulty finding other sufferers. Its growth to a condition that annually afflicts millions exactly parallels the spread of industrialization; doctors may have been the first victims because they used to mix their own medicines, many of which were new chemical compounds. Hayfever offers further confirmation that we cannot expose ourselves, or our environment, to *ad lib* pollution without adversely affecting our health.

We believe that many of the emerging allergic reactions, particularly to food, are caused by the same pollution that directly produces PFR and conditions such as hayfever. They may be attributed to the residues of pesticide sprays and processing chemicals, molecules of which can be found in almost all of our food. Many forms of allergic reaction may be generated by carbon-based molecules in our general environment, exacerbated by forms of pollution now recognized as undesirable, such as vehicle emissions.

Allergic reactions are generated by the body's immune systems. These are complex interactive systems, working at every level within the body, designed to protect it against the effects of foreign invaders and functional errors like the production of cancer cells. To carry out its protective function, the immune system has to be able to identify a vast range of molecules and life-forms. To do this, it has banks of information to which it can refer; we add to one part of this information bank when we become immune to a particular disease. The profile of the disease entity is registered and antibodies are developed to deal with it.

Disease entities are, in general, fairly large and distinct organisms. Our immune system works on the basis of recognition of the protein pattern of their outer coating. It also has to be capable of much finer recognition, focusing down to the molecular level. In hayfever sufferers, pollen grains mistaken for pathogens cause mast cells to degranulate. This degranulation releases a flood of unpleasant chemicals, including histamine, intended to make life unpleasant or impossible for the supposedly dangerous invader. While mast cells remain intact, it is thought that their crystalline structure is analogous to a memory chip, assessing the food and other molecules that constantly pass their strategic sites in the body.

The carbon-based artificial molecules now present in our environment overload these systems, and it only takes a pollen grain to trigger a totally inappropriate response. The subject is more fully dealt with in our book *Hayfever—No Need to Suffer;* the point for the present is that the whole immune system is complex and finely balanced. Like all such systems, the degree to which their function can be stretched without breakdown occurring will be limited.

The liver is the final destination for much of the debris produced by the work of the immune systems. The chemical and biological warfare that the systems produce in response to perceived threats places a load on the liver. Normally this poses no problem; these systems are working all the time, and most of the time we are completely unaware of their activity. Only when we become sick, through a temporary failure or extended battle with an infection, is it brought to our attention. Nevertheless, in susceptible individuals, it is quite feasible that the strain of allergic overload could substantially reduce the body's capacity to deal with toxins arriving from other sources. In such cases PFR is a possible outcome.

The general danger of all the pesticide residues to which we are exposed is that they are capable of affecting almost any level of our being. These substances are designed to work by disrupting the life-form at which they are aimed. They do this principally by punching holes in cell membranes and destroying the integrity of the cell, thereby killing it.

This mechanism has been used for our benefit in the past; it is the way penicillin works. The penicillin molecule becomes incorporated in the bacterial cell during its growth and disrupts the integrity of the structure, making it nonviable. However, as we know, many bacteria have acquired resistance to penicillin; they have done this by learning to take the penicillin molecule apart, rendering it ineffective. Sooner or later, most pest species acquire resistance to the pesticides used against them. Indeed, some seem to bounce back with renewed vigor: the salmonella bacterium, an increasing problem for hospitals and the general population, is one example. It is of growing concern because of the regular dosing of factory-farmed animals with antibiotics. When people eat antibiotic-laden meat, they build up a resistance to the drug. Another example is the super-rat, which now thrives on the warfarin put out as poison.

As the pesticides become more refined, they are deployed against more specialized systems within the target organism; but in their turn, these specialized systems have greater capacity to achieve resistance. Thus a never-ending circle, highly profitable for pesticide manufacturers, is created.

For humans, problems may be accentuated by the fact that our cell membranes are made principally of fatty substances, especially cholesterol. The possible problems caused by the affinity of pesticide for fats become at this point almost infinite.

The organophosphates, the pesticides now predominant in modern farming, are nonpersistent, according to the manufacturers. However, we have been able to find no convincing assurance of their final biodegradability into harmless products in our environment. We suspect that their use is encouraged by a general belief that they simply go away. Because of this, those charged with investigating residue problems tend not to look for these substances or their breakdown products, concentrating instead on less-used insecticides. Many of the breakdown products of pesticides are not even known, and will therefore not be found by the methods of analysis now used. This leaves wide open the possibilities of adverse effects of the widespread use of such substances.

16

The Rest of the Iceberg

This book has concentrated on the problem of unwanted fat caused by toxins in our diet and environment. We named this problem the PFR Syndrome, but as you will have gathered from the previous chapter, it is possible that PFR is simply the identifiable part of a range of other interrelated problems. This chapter is largely speculative—we have no hard evidence to back up the hypotheses we are putting forward, and you may consider them intuitive if you like—but they fit the facts.

That persistent fat that we find so irksome is actually a protective mechanism, shielding our bodies from other possible effects of the substances that cause fat retention. What were these effects, we asked ourselves: what happens to people when the substances to which they are exposed are not dumped into fat? To answer this question, we retraced our steps into toxicology textbooks. And here, in addition to what we were looking for, we also found some recognition of the protective role of fat. In their standard work, *Toxicology: The Basic Science of Poisons*, Casarett and Doull state, "The toxicant while it is stored often does no harm to the organism. Storage depots should therefore be considered as protective organs. . . ." The authors comment that there is a possibility of "a sudden increase in concentration of chemicals in the blood should there occur a rapid mobilization of body fat," but they do not speculate on the consequences of such mobilization.

One extreme consequence was among the clues we had at the beginning of our PFR Syndrome search. Some years ago large numbers of migratory seabirds were found floating, dead, in the North Sea. The cause of death was a mystery for some time; eventually it was attributed to PCBs—polychlorobiphenyls, chemicals used in a great many industrial processes—although how they caused death was unclear. We now know what happened. Migratory birds put on fat to store energy for their long flights. During such flights a rapid mobilization of this body fat occurs, and any substances stored in it are released. These birds must have picked up lethal doses of PCBs, stored them protectively but incidentally in fat, and then released them, with tragic consequences.

Fortunately for humans, our metabolisms are not so simple, nor are we as crucially dependent on cyclic use of fat reserves, so mobilization is not fatal. However, some consequences of uncontrolled mobilization and/or heavy toxic exposure are already apparent in the medical literature, and there is suggestive evidence pointing to more. Disease associated with poisoned fat can affect many systems of the body. Examples come from the effects of crash diets and unaccustomed strenuous exercise, both of which mobilize fat rapidly.

Of all methods of dieting, the very low-calorie, protein-based, weight-loss drinks used to replace all meals are potentially the most harmful. Their success in rapidly metabolizing fat stores is also the source of their danger. There are various forms of such diets; the Cambridge Diet is probably the best known. A book describing the general approach of these diets was published in 1976, written by Robert Linn and titled *The Last Chance Diet*; it was just that for some. According to a report in the *FDA Drug Bulletin*, more than sixty deaths occurred in people consuming liquid-protein diets. It is well known that for each such death attributed by a doctor to the effects of a diet, many more will occur without the cause being recognized. The true death toll due to these diets can never be known. The real number of deaths could run into thousands.

The best-documented result of rapid mobilization of poisoned fat is a heart attack. Ironically, some people launch into drastic diet and exercise regimens in order to avoid heart attacks. The tragic outcome of their efforts results from a failure to recognize the nature of the problem. Controlled studies of very low-calorie, high-protein diets reveal that potentially fatal disturbances of heart rhythm develop quickly. You will now appreciate that, as the liver is directly connected to the heart, this is what may be expected. Whether from drastic diet/exercise regimens or from low-calorie, high-protein diets, the result tends to be the same: a high and sometimes fatal loading on the heart.

The disruption of the body's systems for metabolizing stress hormones when liver glutathione stores are decreased will add to this problem. Very low-calorie diets rapidly deplete the levels of this crucial detoxifying substance. Under these circumstances, stress hormones may build up to levels that damage the heart.

It is easy to see how the media, and many doctors, may periodically be persuaded to launch campaigns against the dangers of exercise. They rarely pick on diets—perhaps because of the multimillion-dollar industry behind dieting. Unfortunately their criticism is generally founded on a prejudice, which they hope will strike a sympathetic chord with their audience, rather than on any real understanding of what is happening in peoples' bodies. When it comes to the positive building of health, their view is lamentably nearsighted.

This nearsightedness is typified by the debate on heart disease and dietary fat—the butter versus margarine controversy. Those who studied causal links between heart disease and diet discovered that a high consumption of saturated fats was associated with increased risk. What they failed to highlight was the fact that these fats tend to be the most heavily contaminated. Heart disease seems to be associated, not with fats as such, but with polluted fats—particularly processed fats. Cholesterol, contrary to popular belief, is harmless, providing it is pure and natural. Other types of fat pollution have yet to be investigated, but we believe that risk to the heart and blood vessels is a feature of many types of contaminants of fats.

Males are more at risk for heart and circulatory disease than females. Hardening of the arteries, where cholesterol is deposited as atheromatous plaques in the blood vessels, seems to be a response of the male metabolism, with its more limited ability to generate toxic adipose tissue. Cholesterol plaques are only dangerous when they degenerate and cause the walls of the blood vessel to ulcerate. We believe that this ulceration is caused by contaminants laid down with the plaque. There are cultures where the diet causes extensive lining of the arteries with cholesterol, but because of its purity, it does not lead to the formation of degenerative plaques or to heart disease. The Masai of Africa, for example, used to live almost exclusively on animal products; people of the Lapp and Innuit cultures ate animals and fish, which used to be free of persistent pesticides.

Recent research has shown that the distribution of fat on the body is important in heart attacks. The person whose waist measurement is very large in relation to hip size has a much higher risk of coronary episodes. This accumulation of belly fat is typical of the PFR Syndrome. Victims can be quite slim apart from a large deposit of fat around the waist; such uneven distribution is a feature of toxic adiposity. So this type of fat deposit, particularly among males, may lead us through toxic input and a limited ability to store in fat, to heart disease as a possible outcome. Heart and circulatory diseases are the most common cause of death in the world; it may be significant that women are not at such high risk until their hormone balance changes after menopause, becoming more like the male's, as do their metabolism and body shape.

Another area of possible problems comes to light with the fact that the molecules stored in adipose deposits would be likely to have a high affinity for other fatty tissues in the body. Such tissues include the nervous system; nerve cells are largely composed of fat. Our brains are 60 percent fat, mostly cholesterol. Clearly we should look for damage to the nervous system; the problem is that low-level disruption may be difficult to detect.

We would expect behavior to be disrupted in a variety of ways, and while this may be easy to observe, it is difficult to link cause and effect in a definite way. However, studies of diet and delinquency have revealed just such a link. Other commentators have pointed to nationwide changes in behavior, such as increased violence and decreasing literacy, and linked such phenomena to environmental chemical pollution.

We do know one case where the circumstantial evidence appears convincing. Kathy suffers from multiple sclerosis, a disease of the fatty tissues that sheathe nerves. She had always been plump; male friends considered her a model of buxom femininity and a happy, lively person. She smoked, and she had three children, none of which influenced her very stable state.

Kathy decided to go on a strict crash diet. Her aim was to shed forty pounds in three months to achieve her target weight. While on this diet, she noticed no obvious ill effects apart from those associated with deliberate self-starvation, such as loss of energy, hunger, and sleeplessness.

The day she decided to strip the varnish from an old sideboard is indelibly fixed in her memory. As she got to work with paint-stripping chemicals, waves of giddiness came over her. Before she could get away, she collapsed. Now she relates the onset of multiple sclerosis to this episode. The combination of crash diet and exposure to a cocktail of chemicals sadly produced the kind of result we would predict.

When Kathy recovered from her collapse, it was some weeks before she realized that something serious had happened to her. At first she did not understand the symptoms; now, five years later, she does not ever expect to be free of multiple sclerosis.

This disease, along with heart disease, is characteristic of our culture. That is to say, it is only found in significant numbers where the Western way of life has spread. Although neither disease has a simple, single cause, both are associated with diets high in sugar and animal fats—precisely the type of diet that we would expect to produce the highest levels of toxic adiposity. The degeneration of the nervous system associated with this diet is, we believe, a consequence of chronic poisoning with fat-soluble toxins.

How many other diseases of the nervous system may result from these ubiquitous hazards? It is of course impossible to say. Not only is there insufficient information to make a reasoned estimate, but the fact that our culture believes that most of these substances are safe inhibits objective research into any diffused effects of this kind.

Two-thirds of the billions of gallons of pesticides sprayed each year are organophosphates. These chemicals are related to nerve gases, yet because of their widespread use, including domestic fly sprays, they are present in the air all the time. The range of accepted symptoms associated with chronic poisoning by this most popular insecticide includes the following: anxiety, uneasiness, emotional instability, giddiness, insomnia, drowsiness, tinnitus (noises, usually ringing, in the ear), inability to get along with family and friends, depression, and weepiness.

These are precisely the symptoms that hundreds of thousands of women suffer all the time in our society. It has been shown that these symptoms can continue for years after exposure to insecticides. These are also the symptoms for which tranquilizers are prescribed, to perhaps 10 percent of the population of the Western world. The cause of the symptoms, and the means of their modification, provide good business for many companies who make both products.

Could it be that we are witnessing nothing less than the population-wide modification of behavior and emotion by our casual use of these substances? It is a theme which has been used in science fiction, but is it really all that far from the truth? We would not wish to imply that such an effect is intentional. And we accept that those charged with regulating the use of such substances may be genuine in their beliefs; but we are equally sure that they are culturally blinkered to the exact nature of such a catastrophe. James Davis, special assistant to the assistant administrator for pesticides and toxic substances at the EPA, confidently asserted in February 1985, "I think we are doing a credible job, and I don't think consumers should be unduly alarmed." At the same time, President Ronald Reagan was promising to get the government off the back of industry. In recent years there has been a decrease in the total number of FDA law-enforcement activities, including seizures, injunctions, prosecutions, and recalls. The current trend harks back to the early years of this century, when food and drug manufacturers were allowed to police themselves. The view expressed by Davis and other government officials is based on the belief that there is little hazard from these insecticides, whether eaten with food or picked up from the general environment. Such a view is clearly nonsense, and depends upon the ignorance of the audience for its acceptance.

The statements of routine complacency mask other hazards. We must go on to consider possible problems associated with changes in fatty tissues. These in turn include diseases linked with female hormones, which are actually produced by fat cells.

The most frightening possible association is with cancer of the breast. Like the other conditions we have mentioned, breast cancer is much more common in developed countries, and it has become increasingly common over the course of this century. Once more it is statistically associated with a diet high in animal fats, and is more common among fatter women. Certain drugs, notably oral contraceptives and the antihypertensive, reserpine, have also been linked to an increased susceptibility to breast cancer.

The female breast is composed largely of fat. The focus of toxins in this fat is clearly indicated by the high level of poisonous residues found in mothers' breast milk, at times rendering it unfit for human consumption, an issue we shall return to later. Unlike most fatty parts of the body, the tissue of the breast is quite active; it undergoes marked changes with the monthly hormonal cycle.

We suspect that the metabolic activity of the natural monthly cycle could produce a situation where toxins stored in breast fat have been put there in error. The aim of storing them on a long-term basis is clearly thwarted by the action of the hormones. Their regular release could mean that they are more likely to trigger local cancers before they can be reabsorbed into fat in other sites.

Animal experiments with drugs and chemicals suggest a special sensitivity of mammary tissues to certain carcinogens. Those that are chemically related to natural female hormones most often induce such cancers. For example, depo-provera, the controversial contraceptive injection, causes mammary tumors in beagles.

At least one in eleven women will develop breast cancer during her lifetime. We cannot be certain of the causes of this epidemic, but almost certainly at least part of the reason for this is our increasing consumption of synthetic hormones, not only in the Pill but also from residues in dairy produce and meat. The other toxic residues are likely to compound the problem. Because of the active nature of breast fat, even those with protective PFR are unlikely to escape. The only solution is to avoid accumulating toxic residues in your body.

Cervical cancer is also hormone-linked, and has also been rising in incidence very rapidly over the past few decades. A direct link with the PFR mechanism is as yet unclear, but the association with smoking suggests that it may be triggered by toxic residues. The induction of the Cytochrome P-450s and the subsequent production of reactive intermediaries may be the key factor. Other contributory elements may be oral contraceptives and poor diet.

Recent increases in skin cancer, associated with white skin exposed to unaccustomed sun, offer another cancer model.

Lately, concern has been focused on the cancer-generating effects of cyclic use of brown-fat reserves. Brown fat is metabolically active fat, sited mainly on the back. It is mobilized by adrenalin to keep us warm under a variety of stresses. If we rely on brown fat for heat generation, its cyclic use could increase the risk of cancer from the release of its contaminants.

Various specialists have estimated that 80 percent of the cancers we now suffer are environmental in origin. Cancer, more than any other condition, is what the body strives to avoid. We all produce faulty, potentially cancerous cells all the time. In the normal course of events, they are recycled by the liver as part of its normal activity. Cancer is stimulated if the detoxification system is overloaded, or if the production of cancer cells outstrips the cleanup capacity of the body. Many of the pesticides and other chemicals discussed in this book not only overload detoxification systems, but have also been shown to be capable of causing cancer.

Typically cancer victims lose weight, sometimes wasting away with horrifying rapidity. As they waste, they develop secondary tumors, frequently in the liver. At this point, the toxic load is overwhelming all the body's coping mechanisms. Quite logically, there are many parallels between the innocent-food diet necessary for escape from PFR and the total organic diet that is advocated as part of the gentle way of curing cancer.

We are convinced that following the PFR escape plan, and weaving its principal elements into your permanent way of life, will not only keep you thin, but will also substantially diminish your risk of developing cancer.

Many women put the health of their children before their own. Some implications of the PFR Syndrome are crucial for anyone who is thinking of having a baby. During pregnancy, all metabolic processes are more active. Fat stores are used by the mother's body to provide for the needs of the developing baby. This will be especially true if she is making efforts to avoid putting on too much weight during pregnancy. Throughout pregnancy the baby will be exposed to the toxins that are being mobilized from its mother's fat. Pesticide residues and other chemicals have been found in the placenta and in the blood of the umbilical cord; it is believed that the fetal liver is involved in the metabolism of these substances. It seems that nature, accepting the limited detoxification capacity of the mother's liver, makes use of the baby's liver also to share the work. There is a logic in this; if the mother were fatally poisoned, the baby would die as well, so they work together to avoid this possibility.

Considering the loading of potential toxins to which the mother is subjected, it is inevitable that her baby is exposed to these residues from its earliest moments of life. And with modern obstetric practices, the fetal liver is sometimes exposed to such a load of drugs that signs of malfunction are apparent at birth.

Neonatal jaundice, once a relatively rare occurrence, reached epidemic proportions at the height of the popularity of birth induction. Even without induction, anesthetics and painkillers given to the mother will reach the baby across the placental wall, stressing its metabolism and detoxification systems.

Newborn babies can have a horrifying range of chemicals circulating in their bloodstreams. One ten-month-old was found to have residues of eight pesticides in his blood, one of which was dieldrin, supposedly banned in most Western countries. His doctor fears long-term damage to the baby's nervous system, including deafness. The doctor treating this baby stated, "It is neither normal nor natural to have pesticides in the blood. A few years ago the high levels I deal with today would have been unthinkable." Another member of the team treating the baby commented, "Fruit and vegetables should carry a government health warning like cigarettes."

After birth, and before the baby can develop any extra coping capacity, the toxic load can build up. Human babies need fat for normal development, and breast milk is 4 percent fat. Unfortunately, this fat contains toxins that have been concentrated by the mother's body. If she has been exposed to high levels of pollution or has an inefficient detoxification system, she may be feeding her baby a concentrated dose of chemicals. All samples of human milk tested in recent years have been found to contain pesticides.

One recent research paper showed that the concentration in breast milk of organic compounds containing chlorine and related substances (halogenated hydrocarbons) can give babies whose mothers are exposed a daily dose in excess of the maximum intake set by the World Health Organization. Babies whose mothers had been exposed to polychlorinated biphenyls at work show high levels of this pollutant in their blood. The chemical remains in the infant's body for several years.

Feeding your baby on cow's milk is not likely to improve the situation. Although cow's milk contains less DDT and other contaminants found in mother's milk, it has a contamination profile of its own. The cow's body concentrates the toxins to which it is subjected, just as the mother's does; these toxins come from chemically sprayed pastures, from the contaminated feedstuffs produced for cattle, and from the increasing numbers of drugs routinely given to animals.

As if this were not bad enough, people are actively exploring new ways of feeding animals that can only add to the problem. Orville Schell's *Modern Meat: Antibiotics, Hormones, and the Pharmaceutical Farm* details just how far this process has gone. Any arguments that we have overstated the issue of contaminated food and its effects may be settled by reference to this book. Among many examples, such as the effect of premature puberty in children produced by overdosing chickens with growth hormones, Schell notes the activities of a waste-reclamation company. They specialize in "exotic feeds for beef and dairy cattle." Among the products this company sells are cardboard, sawdust, ground bark, ground cardboard and grapefruit peel, and various grades of wastepaper—all as cattle feed. Dr. A. H. Peavey comments, "The nutritional value of wastepaper such as newsprint, computer paper, brown shopping bags, and corrugated boxes varies with source . . . and depends on the pulping treatment, source of wood, and additives such as glue, ink, clay, and plastics." If we are prepared to treat our bodies as garbage pails, why not the bodies of other animals?

Some years ago infantile eczema was more common among bottle-fed than breast-fed babies. Today the situation is reversed; breast-fed infants are more likely to suffer this unpleasant allergic condition. The reason is probably the increasing pollution level of mothers' milk.

The problems of your PFR and the risk of passing toxins on to your baby can add a whole new and more realistic view to family planning. Many of the problems for children are avoidable if you detoxify your body, its inputs, and your personal environment, before you conceive. The Plan has all you need. You should stick to YES foods as much as possible, and eat on Schedule I through your pregnancy and while you are breast feeding.

Vegetarian mothers have been shown to have lower chemical-residue levels in their milk. As a consequence, while they keep to a sensible, balanced diet that provides plenty of protein and other nutrients, their babies are healthier.

Hyperactive children present a problem for growing numbers of parents. While we would not go as far as some drug companies, who have a vested interest in describing most children as hyperactive, there is no doubt that it is a condition that afflicts many. It has been convincingly linked with additives in favorite foods, especially coloring and flavoring chemicals. If you have this problem, changing your family over to the detoxifying diet, as you change your eating habits, should help. The health and sociability of your children will improve, and you will avoid the problem of childhood obesity. The addictive nature of many of these substances may make the changeover difficult; you just have to persevere.

Allergic children are often, as we would expect, born to PFR victims. Over the years there have been many TV programs on the problems of allergic and hyperactive children. We now recognize that the mothers, almost without exception, were those heavy, over-rounded types typical of the PFR Syndrome. Because their systems could not cope with chemical loading, they had become fat. During pregnancy the overload was passed on to their babies, damaging their immune systems before birth.

The implications of the PFR Syndrome and its cause are widespread. It is likely that every person on the planet is poisoned to some degree and will also suffer some adverse effect from these substances. It is illogical to demand more medical solutions in an increasingly hazardous environment. We should not accept this situation.

We believe passionately that health should be the first priority of our social and economic systems. To the degree that it is not, and to the degree that those systems actually harm us, they must be judged as failures in meeting human needs. This book, and its plan to help you lose weight caused by toxins in your environment, should not be necessary. That it is should make you angry. Angry enough to add your voice to those who are trying to change the world in which we live for the better. Addresses of organizations campaigning for conservation and environmental improvement can be found in Appendix 5. You may have to step out of line a little, but many others are doing the same thing. Not so long ago, those growers who insisted that organic was best were mocked; advocates of organic agriculture were dismissed as food faddists by those hooked on progress via the techno-fix. You are now in a good position to judge who was right.

The causes of the ill effects on our health that we have been discussing are within our control. Political expediency and profit are the forces that generate the problems; inertia, habit, and ignorance maintain them. The politics of food and environment are increasingly on the agenda in every country in the world, and you have to help keep them there until rational answers are forthcoming. The profit motive is amenable to modification; if enough people stop buying contaminated garbage to eat, sooner or later they will stop making it. Point your purse in the right direction every time you shop.

The only answer to the larger problem is to change the priorities of the major polluters of the world: industry and the agribusiness food producers. The same goes for government. People in government want power; they should hold it only if human welfare is their chief priority.

More than twenty years ago, Rachel Carson's *Silent Spring* sounded a warning that caught people's imagination. Since then the problem has gone underground; we have not learned the essential lesson of that warning. We should have understood that it was necessary to work toward a way of living that enhanced life, rather than one that refined the spraying of death. We need to change the philosophy that accepts such methods, so that organically grown food becomes the norm, rather than a scarce commodity. Pure, unpolluted air, water, and food should be available to everyone, not just to those who search and travel miles to get them.

Appendix 1

Food Additives

The material in this appendix lists additives that are safe, those that are suspect, and those that should be completely avoided.

Colors

Beware	Suspect	Safe
FD&C Yellow No. 5 (tartrazine)	Carminic acid	Turmeric
FD&C Yellow No. 10 (quinoline yellow)	Aluminum	Curcumin
FD&C Yellow No. 6 (orange yellow S)		Riboflavin (vitamin B2)
Azorubine		Lactoflavin
FD&C Red No. 40		Chlorophyll
Cochineal red A		Carbon
FD&C Red No. 3		Carotenes
Patent blue		Anthocyanins
FD&C Blue No. 1		Chalk
FD&C Blue No. 2		Titanium oxide
		Iron oxides and hydroxides

Beware
FD&C Green No.
 3
Carbon Black
Lithol-rubin BK
 (coloring cheese
 rinds)

Preservatives

Beware	Suspect	Safe
Benzoic acid	Formic acid	Sorbic acid
Sodium benzoate	Sodium formate	Thiabendazole
Potassium benzoate	Calcium formate	Acetic acid
	Lactic acid	Potassium acetate
Calcium benzoate	Carbon dioxide	Sodium acetate
Ethyl p-hydroxy-benzoate		Calcium acetate
		Propionic acid
Sodium p-hydroxybenzoate		Sodium propionate
		Calcium propionate
Propyl p-hydroxybenzoate		
Sodium propyl p-hydroxybenzoate		
Methyl p-hydroxybenzoate		
Sulfur dioxide		
Sodium sulfite		
Acid potassium sulfite		
Acid sodium sulfite		
Sodium disulfite		
Potassium disulfite		
Calcium sulfite		

Beware
Calcium disulfite
Diphenly ketone
Orthophenlyphe-
  nol
Sodium
  orthophenyl phenate
Hexamethylenetetramine
  (only in caviar)
Sodium nitrite
Potassium
  nitrite

Notes

1.	Sorbate	From mountain ash berries
2.	Benzoates	Dangerous to asthmatics, hyper-sensitives, and those with allergies.
3.	Sulfur dioxide	Beware of uncooked raw fruit. Dangerous to asthmatics, hypersensitives. Lowers vitamin E content of flour. Lowers vitamin B1 content of various foods.
4.	Biphenyl compounds	Beware of citrus peel. Some probably penetrates inside the fruit.
5.	Lactic acid	Beware in food for very small babies.
6.	Propionate	Migraine sufferers should avoid these.
7.	Carbon dioxide	Enhances absorption in stomach. Increases effect of alcohol.

8. Nitrite   Highly controversial. Many nitrites
                      combine with amines in the stomach,
                      producing cancer-forming
                      nitrosamines. Interacts dangerously
                      with the blood cells of infants.

9. Hexamethyl-   May upset intestine, urinary system,
   enetetramine   or, less often, the skin. Possibly
                      cancer-forming.

Antioxidants, Emulsifiers, Stabilizers, Miscellaneous

Beware	Suspect	Safe
Octyl gallate	Lactates	Ascorbic acid
Dodecyl gallate	Carrageenan	Sodium ascorbate
BHA	Acacia gum	Calcium ascorbate
BHT	Mannitol	Ascrobyl palmitate
Phosphate	Dosodium	Tocopherol-rich
Silicates	tartrate	extracts of natu-
	Dipotassium	ral origin
	tartrate	Synthetic alpha
	Ammonium	tocopherol
	phospatides	Synthetic gamma
	Sodium salts of	tocopheral
	fatty acids	Synthetic delta
	Potassium salts	tocopheral
	of fatty acids	Lecithins
	Calcium salts of	Citric acid
	fatty acids	Calcium citrate
	Monoglycerides	Tartaric acid
	Diglycerides	Neutral potassium
	Acetic acid	tartrate
	Lactic acid	Neutral sodium
	Citric acid	tartrate
	Tartaric acid	Acid potassium
	Sorbitan	tartrate
	monostearate	Sodium potassium
	Chlorides	tartrate

Suspect	Safe
Sulphuric acid	Sodium
Sodium sulphate	orthophosphate
Monoesters of	Potassium
propylene	orthophosphate
glycol	Calcium
Sodium stearoyl-	orthophosphate
2-lactylate	Alginic acid
Calcium stearoyl-	Sodium alginate
2-lactylate	Potassium alginate
Caustic soda	Ammonium
Caustic potash	alginate
Ammonium	Calcium alginate
hydroxide	1,2-propylene glycol
Magnesium	alginate
oxide	Agar-agar
Glucono delta	Carob gum (locust
lactone	bean gum)
Sodium lactate	Guar gum
Potassium	Gum tragacanth
lactate	Gum arabic
Calcium lactate	Sorbitol
	Glycerol
	Pectin
	Methyl cellulose
	Hydroxypropylcellulose
	Methylethylcellulose
	Carboxymethylcellulose
	Potassium sulphate
	Calcium sulphate
	Magnesium
	sulphate
	Calcium hydroxide
	Magnesium
	hydroxide

Safe

Silicone dioxide
Silica
Kaolin

Flavor Enhancers

Beware	Suspect	Safe
Glutamic acid		Beeswax
Monosodium glutamate		Carnauba wax
Monoammonium glutamate		Shellac
Monopotassium glutamate		
Disodium insonate		
Disodium insoninate		
Maltol		
Ethyl maltol		
Chlorine		

Notes

1. Gallates   A benzoate, not permitted in foods intended for young children. May harm asthmatics, those sensitive to aspirin, hyperactive children.
2. Lactates   To be avoided for very young children.
3. EDTA   May disrupt absorption of iron, zinc, and copper.
4. Carrageenan   Irish moss, a seaweed; may cause ulcerative colitis, and may decompose to a carcinogen. Worst in drinks.
5. Acacia gum   Known to be toxic at 100%; some confections get to 45%!

6.	Mannitol	Occasionally produces hypersensitivity.
7.	Stearates	May produce skin allergies; a possible cause of kidney stones.
8.	Polyoxye-thylenes	Very little information available; may alter absorption of fat.
9.	Polyphos-phates	Used to retain moisture in meat products, they can easily be abused to inflate the weight (and price) of a product. Beware particularly of chicken and ham.
10.	Sorbitan esters	Very little information available. May increase intestinal absorption of hydrocarbons, which are irritants.
11.	Chlorides	Several are capable of corrosive effects on the intestine, and perhaps disturbances of body fluids. Very little information available.
12.	Acids and alkalis	These are all corrosive in sufficient quantity. Little information is available as to how they are used.
13.	Ferrocy-anides	We depend for our safety on nothing disturbing their low absorption from the intestine.
14.	Aluminum	Suspected of harming some people.
15.	Bone phos-phate	Vegetarians would wish to avoid this.
16.	Flavor enhancers	Make the food taste better than it really is. Along with salt and sugar, largely responsible for distorting appetites and encouraging overeating. Almost certainly implicated in the epidemic of obesity in young people.

17. Purines	Prohibited from foods intended for young children. Gout sufferers, and rheumatics generally, should avoid these.
18. Hydrocarbons	Liquid paraffins, which as cathartics may cause anal seepage, soreness, and stool looseness, in some people.
19. Bleaches	Doubts exist about safety. In flour, bleach destroys vitamin E and other nutrients. Capable of causing major intestinal upset and convulsions.
20. Fats and soaps	Little information is given. In quantity, could interfere with intestinal function and absorption.
21. Formates	Formic acid very irritating to skin. All have diuretic effects.
22. BHA and BHT	Currently subjects of intensive safety research, because of many doubts. May contribute indirectly to waste of body stores of vitamin D or cause hyperactivity.

Appendix 2

Prescription Drugs That May Cause Weight Gain

This list cannot be exhaustive for two reasons. First, new drugs are being introduced into the market continually and therefore the list will not always be up-to-date. Second, drugs that are capable of inducing weight gain in a minority of people may not yet be known to do so—especially if they cause weight loss in some individuals and gain in others. This is a common pattern with allergic reactions, and many liver-related drug reactions are believed to be associated with allergy.

Drugs named on this list will not cause weight gain in all those who take them. Side effects of drugs are almost always a product of a unique interaction between the nature of the substance and the individual metabolism of the person who takes them. Therefore, any drug you take or have been taking should be regarded as one of the possible causes of your PFR problem.

These lists have been compiled from standard reference sources—Martindale, *The Extra Pharmacopaeia* (London: The Pharmaceutical Press, 1984) and *British National Formulary*. These sources give side effects for whole classes of drugs, and we acknowledge that weight gain may not have been specifically related to all brands listed here. However, since data on changes in weight with each particular product may not be available, while side effects of one member of a drug class are likely to be

188

shared by others in the same class, we have endeavored to include all similar forms. *Note:* Brand names of generic drugs are given in the right-hand columns of the listings that follow.

GROUP 1: HORMONES

Generic drug names: clomiphene citrate, danazol, progesterone, estradiol, estropipate, ethinyl estradiol, ethynodiol diacetate, hydroxyprogesterone caproate, medroxyprogesterone acetate, megestrol acetate, mestranol, norethynodrel, levonorgestrol, quinestrol. Brand products that include these drugs are listed below.

Oral contraceptives (the contraceptive pill): all types.

The Pill can induce a variety of changes in liver function. One important effect is to slow down the action of one of the main detoxifying enzymes, aryl hydrocarbon hydroxylase, which deals with substances such as petrochemicals, by as much as a third. Slow liver function has been demonstrated in overweight women taking the Pill. Abnormal liver function associated with the Pill has been related to severe allergic reactions to foods and chemicals. Recovery after discontinuing Pill use is often slow, but Evening Primrose Oil is helpful.

Contraceptive injections

Medroxyprogesterone acetate   Depo-Provera

Preparations used for hormone replacement therapy and menstrual problems

Ethinyl estradiol	
Estradiol	Brevicon, Modicon, Orthonovum, Ovral, Estrace
Conjugated estrogens	
Premarin	Estrovis
Quinestrol	Danocrine
Progesterone	Progesterone 50
Hydroxyprogesterone caproate	Prodrox 250
Medroxyprogesterone acetate	Depo-Provera, Provera

Male sex hormones and antagonists

Methyltestosterone	Android, Estratest, Metandren
Testosterone	Testosterone
Testosterone cypionate	Depo-Testosterone, T-Cypionate

Other hormones

Clomiphene citrate	Clomid, Serophene

GROUP 2: DRUGS FOR DIABETES

Insulin: any form when dose exceeds requirements

Tolbutamide	Orinase, Tolbutamide
Chlorpropamide	Diabenese, Glucamide
Acetohexamide	Dymelor
Glipizide	Glucotrol
Tolazamide	Tolinase
Glyburide	DiaBeta, Micronase

GROUP 3: DRUGS ACTING ON THE CENTRAL NERVOUS SYSTEM

Antidepressants

Amitriptyline	Elavil, Endep, Triavil, Limbitrol
Desipramine	Pertofrane, Norpramin
Doxepin	Sinequan, Adapin
Imipramine	Tofranil
Maprotiline	Ludiomil
Nortriptyline	Aventyl, Pamelor
Protriptyline	Vivactil
Trazodone	Desyrel
Trimipramine	Surmontil
Phenelzine	Nardil
Isocarboxazid	Marplan
Tranylcypromine	Parnate

Tranquilizers and drugs used for schizophrenia and other psychoses

(Some of these drugs may also be prescribed for nausea, vertigo, Ménière's Disease, and other problems.)

Chlorpromazine	Thorazine
Fluphenazine	Prolixin
Lithium carbonate	Eskalith, Lithane, Lithobid
Lithium citrate	Cibalith-s
Perphenazine	Trilafon, Triavil, Etrafon
Pimozide	Orap
Prochlorperazine	Combid, Compazine
Promazine	Sparine
Thiethylpcrazine	Torecan
Thioridazine	Melleril
Trifluoperazine	Stelazine

Other generic types associated with weight gain include:
loxapine, mesoridazine, molindone, piperacetazine, thiothixene.

GROUP 4: DRUGS FOR PREVENTION OF MIGRAINE

Methysergide	Sausert

(See also Beta-blockers, below.)

GROUP 5: DRUGS FOR HEART DISEASE AND HIGH BLOOD PRESSURE

Beta-blockers
Most drugs of this type, including forms not listed here, are known to precipitate "weight changes." This list includes those which are associated with weight gain.

Atenolol	Tenormin, Tenoretic
Metoprolol	Lopressor
Nadolol	Corgard
Pindolol	Visken
Propranolol	Inderal, Inderal LA
Timolol	Blocadren

Other drugs prescribed for high blood pressure

Clonidine	Catapres
Minoxidil	Loniten
Pargyline	Eutonyl
Reserpine, rauwolfia alkaloids	Harmonyl, Regroton, Rauwiloid, Serpasil, Raudixin

Cholesterol-reducing drugs

Clofibrate	Atromid-S

GROUP 6: ANTI-INFLAMMATORY DRUGS

Indomethacin	Indocin, Indocine SR
Sulindac	Clinoril

GROUP 7: ANTIHISTAMINES

Cyproheptadine	Periactin

Appendix 3

Organic Food Suppliers

MAIL-ORDER SOURCES
Check the labels; some of these companies also market food that is not grown by organic methods.

Arrowhead Mill
P.O. Box 2059
Hereford, TX   79045

Autumn Harvest Natural
  Foods, Ltd
1029 Davis St.
Evanston, IL   60201

Birkett Mills
P.O. Box 440 A
Penn Yan, NY   14527

Butte Creek Mill
402 Royal Ave. N
Eagle Point, OR   97524

Calloway Gardens Country
  Store
Highway 27
Pine Mountain, GA   31822

Erewhon Trading Company
236 Washington St.
Brookline, MA   02146
1-800-222-8028

Fangorn Organic Farm
Rte. 3, Box 141B
Rocky Mount, VA   24151

Flory Brothers
841 Flory Mill Rd.
Lancaster, PA   17601

Four Chimneys Farm Winery
Himrod-On-Seneca, NY
   14842
607-243-7502

Great Valley Mills
Quakertown, PA   18951

Grover Co.
2111 S. Industrial Park Ave.
Temple, AZ 85282

Hodgson Mill Enterprise, Inc.
P.O. Box 126
Gainsville, MO   65655

Homestead Flour
911 W. Camden Rd.
Montgomery, MI   49255

Kenyon's Grist Mill
Usquepaugh, RI   02836

Letoba Farm Foods
Box 180, Rte. 3
Lyons, KS   67554

Mountain Ark Trading
  Company
Fayetteville, AR   72701
1-800-643-8909

New Hope Mills
R.R.2
Moravia, NY   13118

Old Mill of Guilford
Box 623, Rte. 1
Oak Ridge, NC   27310

Shiloh Farms
Box 97, Highway 59
Sulphur Springs, AR   72768

Vermont Country Store
Weston, VT   05161

Walnut Acres
Penns Creek, PA   17862

Wilson Milling Co.
P.O. Box 481
La Cross, KS   67548

RETAIL SUPPLIERS OF ORGANIC FOODS

The stores listed offer organic produce and staples. Many mail-order items on request.

New England
Baldwin Hill Bakery
Baldwin Hill Rd. (off Rte. 2A)
Phillipston, MA   01331
617-249-4691

Good Day Market Cooperative
155 Brackett St.
Portland, ME   04102
207-772-4937

Hartman's Back to Basics
250 Main St.
East Greenwich, RI   02818
401-885-2679

The Whole Grocer
118 Congress St.
Eastern Promenade
Portland, ME   04101
207-774-7711

New York
Commodities
117 Hudson St.
New York, NY   10013
212-334-8330

Laughing Gull Organics
555 North Country Rd.
St. James, NY   11780
516-584-7363

MacDonald's Farm Market and Natural Food Store
2 West Main St.
Trumansburg, NY   14886
607-387-5225

Mid-Atlantic
Earth Things, Inc.
106 Rte. 46
Rockaway, NJ   07866
201-627-4610

Harvestin Natural Foods
12 Locust Lane
Westminster, MD   21157

Valley Health Foods
2571 Huntingdon Pike
Huntingdon Valley, PA   19006
215-947-4585

The Cash Grocer, Inc.
1313 King St.
Alexandria, VA   22314
703-549-9544

The Grow-cery
6526 Landsdowne Ave.
Philadelphia, PA   19151
215-877-5902

Midwest
New City Market
1810 N. Halstead St.
Chicago, IL   60614
312-280-7600

Springfield Community Foods
300 N. Waverly
Springfield, MO   65802
417-866-1337

The Outpost Natural Foods Cooperative
3500 North Holton
Milwaukee, WI   53212
414-961-2597

South
Bread of Life
Health Food Store
1575 NE 26th St.
Fort Lauderdale, FL   33305
305-566-2799

Natural Health Producers
5531 Richmond
Houston, TX   77056
713-783-8444

West
Aline's Natural Foods & Wholesome Living Products
Alpha Beta Plaza, Farmers Lane
Santa Rosa, CA   94505
707-526-4912

Totality House Organic Produce
17 Fourth Ave.
Chula Vista, CA   92010
619-425-2813

Northwest
Whole Earth Exchange
2600 College Rd.
Box 80228
Fairbanks, AK   99708
907-479-2052

Canada
Baldwin Natural Foods
20 1/2 Baldwin St.
Toronto M5T 1L2
Canada
416-979-1777

The Big Carrot
355 Danforth Ave.
Toronto M4K 1N7
Canada
416-466-2129

Appendix 4

Basic Movement

This routine is for those whose range of movement and ability may be severely restricted.

The object is to encourage you to extend your range of movement by progressively increasing the use of muscle groups you might normally ignore. You should not try to do too much at any one time—for you little, but often, is the key. Be cautious if you are very overweight; straining and immobilizing yourself through overexertion is the last thing you want to do. Gradual, steady progress is what you are after. As you become more mobile, you will be able to add more effort, which in turn will increase your mobility. You will have created a positive cycle, which will lead you to success.

Try to do all the movements listed below, but if you can't, don't worry—just do as many as you can for now. You will see that we do not say how many times or how long you should continue each movement. You must judge this. At the start you should stop as soon as you feel tired. Once you have been through the routine a few times, you will learn how much you can manage. Do as much as you can. If you continue while you are enjoying it, that is the best guide. Sooner or later this routine will seem too easy or too boring. Then it has served its purpose, and you are ready to move on to something else!

PREPARATION

For you this may be as demanding as a four-hour workout is for Jack LaLanne, so make sure you are ready. A relaxed and positive state of mind is essential; perhaps some meditation and breathing may be helpful. Wear clothing that is comfortable and will not hinder your movement. Make sure nothing will interrupt or distract you. Have some soft and easy music on if you feel it will help.

Exercise 1. With your feet flat on the floor, stand with your back against a wall. Stretch up and push as much of you against the wall as you can—paying particular attention to getting your shoulders up and back. Once you are in your best position, hold it, and relax and breathe as deeply and slowly as you can. Concentrate on filling yourself up with as much air as you can get in, and let it out slowly. Really feel your chest rise and expand with each breath. Don't worry if your heart knocks a bit or you feel a touch of giddiness—that is just the effect of the load coming off, or the extra oxygen. Keep breathing deeply as long as it feels good, but do at least six really deep and slow ones. While you are in this position search for the feeling in your back and shoulders. Try to identify the feeling so that being upright with your shoulders back becomes your normal way of standing.

Exercise 2. Away from the wall, stand comfortably, with your feet a foot or so apart and your arms loose at your sides. Now just bend your knees a little so that you sink down a few inches—you must judge how far you can do it—then swing your hands up to your shoulders, and reach up as far as you can above your head. As you stretch your arms upward, straighten your legs again, and push up on your toes to reach even higher. Keep your arms straight and lower them to your sides, and come down from your toes. Finally bend your knees again, and repeat. Breathe in as you go up and out as you come down. Move at an easy pace, and try to make it smooth and continuous; don't jerk. Raise and lower your arms both in front and to the sides to add a little variety. Feel what is happening to the parts of you that are moving. You could break this into two movements if necessary, by sitting and doing the arm movement and stretch up, and then standing and doing the leg movement, using the back of a chair for balance if necessary.

Exercise 3. Either seated or standing, as you did the previous movement, reach your arms out straight at the sides at shoulder height. Stretch out as far as you can with your fingertips. Now slowly move your straight arms so that your fingertips go round in small circles. Breathe in as they go up and back, out as they go forward and down. Once you have got the rhythm right, make the circles as big as you can. Keep your back straight and the movement slow and easy, taking the timing from your breathing. You may prefer to start by just letting your arms dangle at your sides and shrugging your shoulders into circles. Breathe the same way when you do this.

Exercise 4. Everyone needs a chair for this one. Stand behind the chair so you can use the back as a support. The movement you are aiming for is to bend forward from the waist, with your legs straight, so that your back becomes parallel with the floor like an ironing board. You may not be able to do that at the beginning, so just bend forward as far as you can, then straighten up, using your hands on the back of the chair as necessary. Concentrate on keeping your back straight throughout. Breathe out, bending forward and in when you straighten up. Slow and easy, once more. Don't go too far at first.

Exercise 5. Lie on your back. A firm surface with a carpet is best. Arms by your sides, feet a little apart. One leg at a time, bring your knee up until your thigh is pointing straight up. Don't try to keep your leg straight, just let your foot dangle. Then lower your knee and straighten out your leg. Repeat for both legs, breathing out as you raise your knee and in as you lower it. Later on you could try swinging your foot up to straighten your leg once your thigh is vertical.

Exercise 6. Same position. Stretch your arms up above your head, with arms straight so that you point to the ceiling. Then lower them back behind your head. Breathe out as you raise and in as you lower. For variety, you can do the same movement to the sides, instead of above your head. Or you could begin by stretching your arms out to the sides, and bending them up first at the elbow, then pushing up toward the ceiling.

Have a few relaxing deep breaths while you are lying on your back. Then when you are ready, complete your session by getting up and going for a walk. You should aim for steady continuous movement, slow if necessary. Shoulders back (remember the wall feeling), swing your arms, loose and smooth. Don't worry about how far or fast, just enjoy the sensation of movement. Afterwards have a treat; perhaps a bath or shower.

As you become more active you will increase the range of movement you can manage. This routine allows for that. When doing Exercise 2 you could end up doing full squats, and then leaping in the air. Exercise 4 could have you touching your toes, and Exercise 5 could turn into leg raises energetic enough for the flattest tummy.

But for now concentrate on enjoying moving. Do a session whenever you feel like it during the day. As you do more, you will discover that it has a positive reinforcing effect. At first you should do it when you feel good, but soon you will discover that being active when you do not feel good will actually change your state—it will make you feel better. Once you make this discovery, you have taken the first step in achieving real control over your body and self.

When you are ready to move on to something else, start thinking about dance. It can provide energetic and enjoyable movement for the whole body.

DANCE

We want you to think about dance as one of the oldest forms of human recreation (re-creation). Dance has always fulfilled a variety of needs: self-expression, relaxation, transcendence, communication, and a number of other emotional needs. Our mundane world limits this advantageous activity mainly to the young. This is wrong. All ages need to regain the innate benefits of dance.

Do not believe you are too old, too fat, too awkward, or too ugly. None of that is important. You may be self-conscious, most of us are. But dance can turn and twist that into something more valuable: consciousness of self.

There are two routes to dance. One is to become totally conscious of every part of your body, to direct each movement and posture and timing; this is the method of the professional dancer. The other is to feel every part of your being; to evolve movement as a partnership between the facets of your self, let your body influence its own direction with your mind as the means.

Take the feeling route. Try to let movement slide into you, using music as the stimulus. Movement should pervade and persuade you, take you along. Let go. Let it take you wherever it will! It may be a soft, sensuous experience or a driving, physical expression of feeling.

Dance can regenerate the very core of your being. Because it is a self-directed activity, it will involve many levels of being, both physical and mental, in creating feedback loops. These can build up sensations and energy, becoming almost frighteningly exhilarating, or become just a gentle exploration of part of your self. Either way, the ancient rhythms will help you unlock and grow.

How do you do it?

To begin with, you will start with simple conscious movements to suitable music, copying the way you've seen others move. Think of all the dance from cultures around the world: Latin American or Hawaiian, perhaps. Don't let yourself be limited by our society's assumptions about dance.

You may find it easier if you watch yourself in a large mirror— but not if the mirror puts you off! You may want to introduce some of the jogging/jumping movements you do as exercise. Fine. While you are moving, try to relax enough to let your body take over. The music should help. Listen to it, let your body go.

Think carefully when you choose your dancing music. You should select something that speaks to you personally, that communicates directly with your being. It could be anything from a Beethoven quartet to the Rolling Stones; it could be punk or romantic, or even disco dancing music. The crucial thing is that it moves you, and you move with it.

Don't be disheartened if nothing magical happens. Enjoy the music and the movement, and sooner or later it will.

Dance as long and as often as you like, alone or in company. See if you can get a partner to join in sometimes. But remember, you are dancing for yourself.

Appendix 5

Organizations Working Toward an Unpolluted World

Action on Smoking and Health (ASH)
2013 H. St. NW
Washington, DC   20006

Center for Science in the Public Interest
1501 16th St. NW
Washington, DC   20036

Consumer Education Research Center
439 Clark St.
South Orange, NJ 07079

Environmental Defense Fund
444 Park Ave. South
New York, NY   10016

Friends of the Earth Foundation
1045 Sansome St.
San Francisco, CA   94111

Greenpeace USA
2007 R. St. NW
Washington, DC   20009

Natural Resources Defense Council
122 E. 42nd St.
New York, NY   10168

Public Citizen Forum
P.O. Box 10404
Washington, DC   20036

Regenerative Agriculture Association
222 Main St.
Emmaus, PA   18049

Soil Conservation Society of America
7515 N.E. Ankeny Rd.
Ankeny, IA   50021

The E.F. Shumacher Society
Box 76 RFD #3
Great Barrington, MA   01230

Appendix 6

Further Help

This book is intended to enable you to safely lose your persistent fat, cellulite, or troublesome flab. We want you to succeed in that objective.

The method described in The Plan is based upon our experience in assisting clients of Life Profile with the same problems—we know that it works. However, because of the wide variability produced by individual differences, life-style, and circumstances, some readers may have specific difficulties, or reach a sticking point that is peculiar to them. To help in these cases, we have produced a special program, within the Life Profile system, which is available to readers of this book.

If you would like to take advantage of this, this is what you should do.

1. Write a summary of the action you have taken so far in following The Plan. Note particular difficulties you have experienced, and also the successes you have had.

2. Give a basic personal outline. We need the following: your age, sex, brief medical and natal history, occupation, weight loss, and weight history. Additionally, we would like you to outline a typical day in your life, and tell us your likes and dislikes, your loves and hates.

3. If you have any thoughts or feelings about a particular difficulty, let us know.

Write to us at the following address:

Life Profile Ltd.,
37b New Cavendish Street
London W1
England

References

Abbott, D. C., et al. "Organochlorine Pesticide Residues in Human Fat in the United Kingdom, 1976–77." *British Medical Journal* (November 1981): 1425–28.

Adam, K., and Oswald, I. "Sleep Helps Healing." *British Medical Journal* (November 1984): 1400–01.

Agricultural Research Council/Medical Research Council. *Food and Nutrition Research.* HMSO, 1974, pp. 160–72.

Arenillas, L. "Amitriptyline and Body-Weight." *The Lancet* (February 1964): 432–33.

Beller, A. S. *Fat and Thin.* Farrar, Straus & Giroux, 1977.

Berko, L. R. *Food Additives Explained: What Those Long Names on Food Labels Tell Us.* Consumer Education Food Task Force, 1983.

Bird, A. G. "Allergic Reactions During Anaesthesia." *Adverse Drug Reaction Bulletin* (February 1985): 408–11.

Bourne, W. R. P. "Seabirds and Pollution." In *Marine Pollution.* Edited by R. Johnson. Academic Press, 1977.

Bray, G. A. "Definition, Measurement and Classification of the Syndromes of Obesity." *International Journal of Obesity* 2 (1978): 99–112.

British Medical Association and Pharmaceutical Society of Great Britain. *British National Formulary.* The Pharmaceutical Press, 1984.

Byrivers, P. *Goodbye to Arthritis.* Century, 1985.

Cannon, G., and Einzig, H. *Dieting Makes You Fat.* Sphere, 1984.

207

Carson, Rachel. *Silent Spring*. Houghton Mifflin, 1962; Fawcett, 1978 (paperback).

Center for Science in the Public Interest. Edited by A. Fritsch. *The Household Pollutants Guide*. Anchor Books, 1978.

Center for Study of Responsive Law. *Eating Clean Food Safely and the Chemical Harvest. Selected Readings.*

Community Nutrition Institute. "Inspection Programs Hit by Spending Cuts." *Nutrition Week* 16 (February 20, 1986).

Community Nutrition Institute. "Food Poisoning Risk: Major Regulatory Issue." *Nutrition Week* 16 (March 27, 1986).

Consumers' Association. "E-Numbers, Doctors and Patients: Food for Thought." *Drug & Therapeutics Bulletin* 22 (1984): 41–42.

Dahlgren, B. E. "Hepatic and Renal Effects of Low Concentrations of Methoxyflurane in Delivery Ward Personnel." *Journal of Occupational Medicine* 22 (1980): 817–19.

Denning, J. "The Hazards of Women's Work." *New Scientist* (January 1985): 12–15.

Denning, J. *Women's Work and Health Hazards: A Bibliography*. Trades Union Council/London School of Hygiene and Tropical Medicine, 1984.

Doull, J., et al., eds. *Casarett and Doull's Toxicology, The Basic Science of Poisons*. Macmillan, 1980.

Erlichman, J. "Good Enough to Eat?" *New Health* (June 1985): 28–33.

Eyton, A. *The F-Plan Diet*. Crown, 1983.

Forbes, A. *The Bristol Diet*. Century, 1984.

Friedman, R. B. "Fad Diets: Evaluation of Five Common Types." *Postgraduate Medicine* 79 (January 1986): 249.

Garner, D., et al. "Cultural Expectations of Thinness in Women." *Psychological Reports* 47 (1980): 483–91.

Gear, A. *The Organic Food Guide*. Henry Doubleday Research Association, 1983.

Gillman, A. G., et al., eds. *Goodman & Gillman's The Pharmaceutical Basis of Therapeutics*. 6th ed. Macmillan, 1980, chapter 1.

Goulding, R. "Chemical Hazards in the Home and Workplace." *Practitioner* 227 (1983): 1363–69.

Grant, E. *The Bitter Pill: How Safe Is the "Perfect Contraceptive"?* Elm Tree Books, 1985.

Hanssen, M. *E for Additives*. Thorsons, 1984.

Hildyard, N. *Cover Up: The Facts They Don't Want You to Know*. New English Library, 1981.

Kendler, K. S. "Amitriptyline-Induced Obesity in Anorexia Nervosa: A

Case Report." *American Journal of Psychiatry* 135 (1978): 1107–08.

Kenton, L., and Kenton, S. *Raw Energy*. Century, 1985.

Lappe, F. M. *Diet for a Small Planet*. Ballantine, 1982.

Laseter, J. L. "Body Burden and Sources of Toxic Volatile Organics." Paper read at the McCarrison Society Conference, 1984. (Cassette available from the McCarrison Society, c/o Margaret Clark, Hon. Sec., 36 Bowners Ave., Oxford OX3 OAL, England.)

Lawrence, F. "Additives Anonymous." *New Health* (April 1985): 30–35.

Lee, D. H. K., ed. "Reactions to Environmental Agents," section 9 in *Handbook of Physiology*. American Physiological Society, 1977.

Mackarness, R. *Eating Dangerously*. Harcourt Brace, 1976.

———. *Not All in the Mind*. Pan, 1976.

———. *Chemical Victims*. Pan, 1980.

Martindale. *The Extra Pharmacopaeia*. The Pharmaceutical Press, 1984.

Melville, A., and Johnson, C. *Cured to Death: The Effects of Prescription Drugs*. Secker & Warburg, 1982.

Millstone, E. "Food Additives: A Technology Out of Control?" *New Scientist* (October 1984): 20–24.

Morley, J. E., and Levine, A. S. "The Central Control of Appetite." *The Lancet* (February 1983): 398–401.

Morse, D. L., et al. "Cut Flowers: A Potential Pesticide Hazard." *American Journal of Public Health* 69 (1979): 53–56.

Murray, A. J., and Portmann, J. E. *Aquatic Environment Monitoring Report*, No. 10.

Ministry of Agriculture, Fisheries, and Food. *Household Food Consumption and Expenditure*. HMSO, 1984.

Ministry of Agriculture, Fisheries, and Food. Directorate of Fisheries Research, 1984.

Nakra, B. R. S., et al. "Amitriptyline and Weight Gain: A Biochemical and Endocrinological Study." *Current Medical Research and Opinion* 4 (1977): 602–06.

Nicolson, R. S. "Surveys of Pesticide Residues in Food, 1983." *Journal of the Association of Public Analysts* 22 (1984): 51–57.

Nutrition Reviews 43 (February 1985): 33–40.

Orbach, S. *Fat Is a Feminist Issue*. Berkley Publishers, 1984.

Paykel, E. S., et al. "Amitriptyline, Weight Gain and Carbohydrate Craving: A Side Effect." *British Journal of Psychiatry* 123 (1973): 501–07.

Paul, A. A., and Southgate, D. A. T. *McCance & Widdowson's The Composition of Foods.* HMSO, 1978.

Polishuk, Z. W. "Effects of Pregnancy on Storage of Organochlorine Pesticides." *Archives of Environmental Health* 20 (1970): 215–17.

Rose, C. "Pesticides: The First Incidents Report." Friends of the Earth, 1081.

Royal Canadian Air Force Exercise Plans for Physical Fitness. Pocket Books, 1972.

Royal College of Physicians. "Obesity." *Journal of the Royal College of Physicians* (January 1983).

Royal College of Physicians and British Nutrition Foundation. "Food Intolerance and Food Aversion." *Journal of the Royal College of Physicians* 18 (1984): 83–123.

Ruckpaul, K., ed. *Cytochrome P-450.* Academic-Verlag, 1984.

Schauss, A. *Diet, Crime and Delinquency.* Parker House, 1981.

Schell, O. *Modern Meat: Antibiotics, Hormones, and the Pharmaceutical Farm.* Random House, 1984.

Soil Association. "Wholefoods May Give You More Than You Bargained For." *Soil Association Quarterly Review* (Winter 1982–83): 7–8.

Steele, G., et al. "Estimates of the Biologic Half-Life of Polychlorinated Biphenyls in Human Serum." *New England Journal of Medicine* 314 (April 3, 1986).

Stellman, J. M., and Daum, S. M. *Work Is Dangerous to Your Health.* Vintage Books, 1973.

Sterling, et al. "Building Illness in the White-Collar Workplace." *International Journal of Health Services* 13 (1983): 277–87.

U.S. Department of Agriculture. *Fact Book of U.S. Agriculture, 1985.* Misc. Pub. No. 1063.

Waldbott, G. C. *Health Effects of Environmental Pollutants.* C. V. Mosby, 1973.

Watts, J. *An Investigation into the Use and Effects of Pesticides in the UK.* Friends of the Earth, 1985.

Wolff, M. S. "Occupationally Derived Chemicals in Breast Milk." *American Journal of Industrial Medicine* 4 (1983): 259–81.

World Health Organization. *Pesticide Residue Series,* Nos. 1–5. World Health Organization, 1972–76.

Acknowledgments

Many people have helped us with this book. We cannot name those in official positions who gave off-the-record information, but nevertheless we thank them. We would like to express our gratitude to those Life Profile clients whose experience we have drawn upon to develop the theory and illustrate the text.

Our special thanks are due to Dr. John Watts, who shared a wealth of information and expertise with us and contributed to discussions of the PFR phenomenon. Dr. Chris Upton and Peter Bunyard each gave generously of both time and knowledge.

We are grateful to Crown Publishers Inc., particularly their senior editor, Lisa Healy, for the enthusiasm brought to this book.

Finally we would like to acknowledge the cheerful persistence and encouragement of our agent, David Grossman, throughout the conception, gestation, and birth of this book.

INDEX

acetaminophen (Tylenol), 159
Action on Smoking and Health, 119
activity plateau, 132–133
adrenalin, 131, 156
advertising, food, 76–77
age:
    metabolism and, 150
    The Plan and, 82
Agriculture Department, U.S. (USDA), 62
Alar (daminozide), 66
alcohol, 40, 41, 49, 50, 77
    liver and, 26, 29, 78
    in PFR diet, 106–107
allergies, 30, 45–47, 50, 163–164
    food, 30, 46, 163–164
    gas stoves and, 116
    hayfever, 30, 41, 46, 58, 76, 163, 164
amaranth (FD&C Red No. 2), 58
American Cancer Society, 119
American Heart Association, 119
amino acids, 93, 94, 156

ammonia, 157
animals, factory farming of, 66–67
animal tests, 57
anorexia nervosa, 15
antibiotics, 67
antidepressants, 36–39, 43–44, 190
antihistamines, 47, 58, 192
anti-inflammatory drugs, 40, 192
antioxidants, 58–59, 183–185
Arrowhead Mills, 90
arthritis, 30, 40–41
asthma, 30, 41–42, 46
    sulfites and, 59
Asthma and Allergy Foundation, 58
Autumn Harvest Natural Foods, 90

baked goods, 58, 85
barbiturates, 159–160
basic movement, 127, 198–202
    dance and, 201–202
    preparation for, 199–201
behavioral changes, 170–171, 172

benzoates, 59
beta-blockers, 191
BHA, 58
BHT, 58–59
bile, 24, 50, 155–156
    pigments, 157
blood, 24, 156
body shape, 71
    deciding on, 150–151
    heat loss and, 18
    permanent good, 148–154
brain, 35, 170
Bray, G. A., 11
brazil nuts, 93
bread, 85, 90
breast cancer, 173–174
breastfeeding, 65, 130, 176, 177
breathing, 124–126, 134
    in week-by-week action plans, 140–144
British Industrial Biological Research Association (BIBRA), 57
British Royal College of Physicians, 11
brown fat, 18, 174

213

California, 65
  pesticide analysis in,
    63
calorie consumption:
  decline in, 8
  seasonal variations in,
    17
Cambridge Diet, 168
cancer, 62, 66–67, 160,
    173–175
  PVC and, 115
Cannon, Geoffrey, 6
carbohydrates, 46–47
  digestion of, 23, 156
carbon monoxide, 125,
    158
carbon-ring systems, 49
Carson, Rachel, 64, 179
*Casarett and Doull's
  Toxicology,*
    167–168
Centers for Disease
  Control, 65, 67
cervical cancer, 174
cheese, 85
children:
  obesity in, 11
  toxins and, 175–178
"Chinese restaurant
  syndrome," 60
chloracne, 65
chocolate, 105
cholesterol, 165, 170
cholesterol-reducing
  drugs, 192
cigarettes, *see* smoking
cirrhosis of the liver, 26,
    65, 162
cleaning, 113–116
clothing:
  cleaning of, 113–114
  exercise and, 127
coffee, 105
colas, 105–106
coloring of food, 58,
    180–181
contraceptive injections,
    189
Cured to Death (Melville
  and Johnson), 7
cysteine, 93, 94
Cytochrome P–450 (C
  P–450s), 158–161,
    174

dairy products, in PFR
  diet, 87, 99, 101,
    106

daminozide (alar), 66
dance, dancing, 127,
    129, 132, 134,
    201–202
Davis, James, 172, 173
DDE, 64
DDT (dichlorodiphenyl-
  trichloroethane), 18,
    64, 176
  in arctic seals, 7, 23
Delaney Clause
  amendment (1958),
    56, 61
Denham, Christopher,
    41–42, 45–46
depression, 36–37, 58,
    65
detoxification, 27, 45,
    50
  of environment, *see*
    environment
  food and, *see* diet,
    PFR
  of home, 78
  in The Plan, 72–73,
    75–78
  in week-by-week
    action plans,
    139–140
diabetes, drugs for,
    190
dieldrin, 64, 175–176
diet, PFR, 83–107
  additives avoided in,
    84–86
  aims of, 83–84
  application of
    principles of, 94–95
  nutrients to select in,
    91–94
  pesticide residues
    avoided in, 86–91
  Schedule I in, 95,
    100, 102–107, 126,
    142–143, 144
  Schedule II in, 95,
    100, 104–107, 144,
    145, 146
  in week-by-week
    action plans, 138,
    139, 141–146
Dieting Makes You Fat
  (Cannon and
  Einzig), 6, 7, 38
diets, dieting, 168
  diminishing returns
    and, 19
  elimination, 76

diets (*cont.*)
  failure of, 9, 10, 20,
    81
  increase in, 8–9
  loss of lean tissue
    during, 25–26
  sexuality and, 15
  successful, 32–34
  in winter, 17–18
digestion, 23–25, 156,
    157
dioxin, 64–65
Doull, J., 167–168
drinks, 105–107
  food additives in, 59
drugs, 24, 29, 54, 57,
    74, 77, 140,
    188–192
  for allergies, 47, 58,
    192
  antidepressants,
    36–39, 43–44, 190
  antihistamines, 47,
    58, 192
  anti-inflammatories,
    40, 192
  central nervous
    system and,
    190–191
  for diabetes, 190
  food additives and
    pesticides compared
    with, 57, 62–63
  for heart disease,
    191–192
  for high blood
    pressure, 191–192
  hormones, 189–190
  livestock and, 66–67
  for migraines, 191
  pregnancy and, 30
dry-cleaning, 114

East West Journal, 90
Eating Dangerously
  (Mackarness),
    46–47
eczema, 30, 46, 177
effort hangover, 38, 44
eggs, in PFR diet, 87–88
Einzig, Hetty, 6, 38
emotions, eating and,
    34
emulsifiers, 183–185
endrin, 64
energy needs, of women,
    149–150
energy storage, 34, 132,
    156

environment, 102–121, 157
 cigarette smoking and, 118–119
 cleaning and, 113–116
 home, 109–119
 insect removal and, 116–117
 pesticide effects and, 64
 repairs and, 117–118
 washing and, 113–114
 week-by-week action plans and, 139–141, 143, 147
 work, 119–121
Environmental Conservation, Department of, 65
Environmental Protection Agency (EPA), 60–63, 65, 66
enzyme systems, Cytochrome P–450, 158–161
Erewhon Trading Company, 89
ergotamine, 54
exercise, 38
 activity plateau and, 132–133
 basic movement, 127, 198–202
 failure of, 9
 increase in, 9
 permanent good shape and, 151–153
 warming up and, 126–130
 in week-by-week action plans, 138, 140–147

fat, body, 13–27
 brown (brown adipose tissue), 18, 174
 cholesterol, 165, 170
 functions of, 13–27
 as insulation, 14, 16–18, 34
 liver and, 24–25
 mobilizing of, 73, 79–82, 130–136, 145–146

fat (*cont.*)
 revving up and, 80, 123, 130–136
 sexual attraction and, 14–16, 20, 21, 34–35
 toxins stored in, 14, 22–27, 161–162, 167–178
Fat Is a Feminist Issue (Orbach), 72
fats, dietary, digestion of, 23, 156
fatty acids, 23
FDA Drug Bulletin, 168
Federal Food, Drug and Cosmetic Act (1938), 55–56
Federal Insecticide, Fungicide, and Rodenticide Act, 62
Feldman, Jay, 60
"female" eating pattern, 149–150
fish:
 pesticide residues in, 54–55, 65
 in PFR diet, 87
flavor enhancers, 59–60, 185–187
flavorings, 56
flours, 85, 90
folic acid, 2
food, 52–68
 advertising of, 76–77
 cysteine and methionine in, 93, 94
 folic-acid-rich, 93
 industrialization of, 54–55, 61–62
 innocent, 76, 83–107
 iron-rich, 92
 labeling of, 60
 natural toxins in, 53–54
 organic, 86, 92–93, 193–197
 PERHAPS, 99
 prepared, 84–85
 processed, 92
 spoilage of, 84
 vitamin C in, 93, 94
 YES, 96–98
 see also diet, PFR; diets, dieting

food additives, 24, 48–49, 55–60, 76, 77, 180–187
 antioxidants, emulsifiers, stabilizers, miscellaneous, 58–59, 183–185
 avoiding, 84–86
 colors, 58, 180–181
 drugs compared with, 57, 62–63
 flavor enhancers, 59–60, 185–187
 preservatives, 59, 181–183
 safety of, 55–57
 testing of, 57
 types of, 58–60
Food and Drug Administration (FDA), 56, 58–59, 62–67, 172
food poisoning, 62, 67
Food Safety and Inspection Service (FSIS), 67
food storage, fat as, 14, 19–22
footwear, 127–128
formaldehyde, 49
formaldehyde-urea foam insulation, 115–116
Four Chimneys Farm wine, 106–107
fruit:
 dried, 59
 pesticides and, 61, 63, 65, 66
fungal poisons, 54
fungicides, 61

gardening, 90
gas stoves, 116
glucose, 23, 156
glutamates, 59–60
glutathione, 26, 159
glycerol, 23
glycogen, 23, 79, 130, 131–132, 135, 156
GRAS (generally recognized as safe) food additives, 56
Green Revolution, 53

hair loss, 29
"hangover" effect, 80, 128, 131, 135

Hanssen, Maurice, 58
hayfever, 30, 41, 46, 58,
76, 163, 164
*Hayfever—No Need to
Suffer* (Melville and
Johnson), 164
headaches, 58
heart, 20
heart disease, 169–170,
171
drugs for, 191–192
hemoglobin, 125
hepatic portal vein, 24,
155
hepatitis, 50
herbicides, 61, 64
high blood pressure,
drugs for, 191–192
home environment,
109–119
hormones, 150, 157
Cytochrome P–450
and, 160–161
drugs and, 189–190
metabolism of,
160–161
hospitals,
environmental
toxins in, 120
"Human Food Safety
and the Regulation
of Animal Drugs,"
66–67

illness, The Plan and, 74
immune system, 29, 30,
46, 164
individual differences:
in metabolism, 109
The Plan and, 70
induction, 160
insects, getting rid of,
116–117
insulation:
fat as, 14, 16–18, 34
formaldehyde-urea
foam, 115–116
insulin rebound, 85–86
*International Journal of
Obesity*, 11
intestines, 155, 156,
157
iron, 92, 157

Jackson, Beth, 39–41,
44–45
jaundice, 50, 175
juices, 105

Kenton, Leslie and
Susannah, 88–89
kidneys, 20, 24, 30, 58,
162–163

laboratories,
environmental
toxins in, 120
Last Chance Diet, The
(Linn), 168
Life Profile Ltd., 5, 7,
22, 38, 206
Linn, Robert, 168
liver (body organ), 20,
21, 23–26, 29, 30,
49–51, 58, 65
alcohol and, 26, 29,
78
cirrhosis of, 26, 65,
162
Cytochrome P–450
and, 158–161
diseases of, 50, 115
failure of, 159
female, 79, 149–150,
156
functions of, 23, 51,
155–157
glycogen storage in,
23, 79, 130, 135,
156
illness and, 74
lobules of, 156, 157,
158
male, 79, 156
nicotine and, 119
regeneration of,
78–79, 83, 124–
125
as warehouse, 23–24,
157
liver (food), 86, 92

Mackarness, Richard,
46–47
maintenance, week-by-
week action plans
and, 146–147
massage, 134
meat:
food additives in, 59
organ, 86, 92
pesticide residues in,
66–67, 165
in PFR diet, 86–87,
99, 101
processed, 66–67
meditation, 124–125

menus, Schedule I, 100,
102
metabolism, 73, 78–79,
109, 122–136
age and, 150
of hormones, 160–161
recovery and,
122–126
revving up and, 80,
123, 130–136
toxic products of, 157
of toxins, 157–159
warming up and, 122,
126–130
Metcalfe, Dean D., 58
methionine, 93, 94
methylene blue, 66–67
migraines, drugs for,
191
Millstone, Eric, 57
minerals, 92–93
liver's storage of,
156–157
mitochondria, 158
Modern Meat (Schell),
176–177
monosodium glutamate
(MSG), 59–60
motivation, 70–72
Mott, Laurie, 60
Mountain Ark Trading
Company, 89–90
multiple sclerosis, 171
muscles, 79–80,
151–153

nails, brittle, 29
National Institutes of
Health (NIH), 58
Natural Resources
Defense Council
(NRDC), 63
neonatal jaundice, 175
nervous system, 35, 65,
155, 157, 170–172
drugs and, 190–191
newborns, chemicals in
bloodstreams of,
175–176
nicotine, 119, 125
nitrates, 59, 67
nitrites, 59
NO foods, 100, 101
Nutrition Reviews, 11

obesity:
causes of, 10–11
in children, 11

obesity (*cont.*)
 increase in, 10
 psychological aspects
  of, 71
offices, environmental
 toxins in, 120
oral contraceptives, 189
Orbach, Suzie, 72
organic food, 86, 92–93
 suppliers of, 193–197
organ meats, 86, 92
organophosphates, 166,
 172
oxygen, 124–125, 159

Pasteur, Louis, 54
PCBs (polychlorinated
 biphenyls), 65, 168,
 176
Peavey, A. H., 177
penicillin, 165
perfumes, 115
PERHAPS Foods, 99,
 100
permanent good shape,
 148–154
 advantages of, 150
 balanced way of life
  and, 154
 exercise and, 151–153
 personal relationships
  and, 153–154
Persistent Fat Retention
 (PFR) Syndrome,
 1–7
 case histories of,
  36–42
 causes of, 29, 43–51
 defined and described,
  28–35
 diet and, *see* diet,
  PFR
 escaping from, *see*
  detoxification;
  metabolism; Plan,
  The
 liver tissue loss and,
  21
 questionnaire, 2–3
 susceptibility to, 26,
  31–32, 50
 symptoms of, 29, 32
 theoretical model of,
  see theoretical
  model of PFR
 *see also specific
  topics*
personal relationships,
 70, 153–154

pesticides, 41, 46, 48,
 60–66, 77–78,
 163–166
 Alar (daminozide), 66
 avoiding residues of,
  86–91
 children and,
  175–177
 cost of, 54
 dioxin, 64–65
 environmental effects
  of, 64
 organophosphates,
  166, 172
 PCBs, 65, 168, 176
 poisoning from, 65
PFR Syndrome, *see*
 Persistent Fat
 Retention Syndrome
Phillips, Amanda,
 36–39, 43–44, 45
Physical Fitness, 152
Plan, The, 69–82
 age and, 82
 detoxification in,
  72–73, 75–78; *see
  also* detoxification
 further help with,
  205–206
 illness and, 74
 metabolic capacity
  increased in, 73,
  78–79, 122–130;
  see also metabolism
 mobilizing fat in, 73,
  79–82, 130–136
 time required for, 82
plastics, 115
poisons, *see* toxins
pollution, 41–42, 76
 organizations working
  against, 203–204
 see also environment
polycyclic hydrocarbons,
 160
pregnancy, 20, 30, 130,
 175
preparatory action plan,
 138–139
preservatives, in food,
 59, 181–183
protein:
 digestion of, 22
 in PFR diet, 86–88
 synthesis of, 156
 vegetable, 88
psych-up, 70, 139
PVC, 115

questionnaires:
 on environmental
  toxins, 109–113
 on PFR Syndrome,
  2–3

rashes, 29, 58
Raw Energy (Kenton
 and Kenton), 89,
 103
Reagan, Ronald, 172
recovery, 78, 122–126
 objectives of, 126
 in week-by-week
  action plans,
  140–142
reproduction, 30
 fat storage and, 19–20
rest, 124
 in week-by-week
  action plans, 138,
  140–145
revving up, 80, 123,
  130–136
 in week-by-week
  action plans,
  144–145
Royal Canadian Air
 Force, 152
running, 133–134

salads, 88
salmonella, 67
Schedule I, 95, 100,
 102–107, 126
 drinks in, 105–107
 menu creation in,
  100, 102
 in week-by-week
  action plans,
  142–143, 144
Schedule II, 95, 100,
 104–107
 drinks in, 105–107
 in week-by-week
  action plans, 144,
  145, 146
Schell, Orville, 176–177
selenium, 92, 93
sexual attraction, fat
 and, 14–16, 20, 21,
 34–35
"sick building
 syndrome," 120
Silent Spring (Carson),
 64, 179
skin cancer, 174
Slaney, Mary Decker, 35

sleep, 124
smoking, 57, 77,
    118–119, 158
    Cytochrome P–450
        and, 160
soft drinks, 105–106
sprouting, 88–89, 93
stabilizers, 183–185
steroids, 47
stress, 140
    hormones and,
        160–161
    minimizing, 124
    recovery and, 124
    winter dieting and,
        17–18
sugar, 85–86
sulfites, 59

tartrazine (FD&C Yellow
    No. 5), 58
teas, herb, 105
Temik (aldicarb
    sulfoxide), 65
theoretical model of
    PFR, 155–166
    Cytochrome P–450
        and, 158–161
thinness, 26–27
    as optimal state, 10
toxic adipose tissue
    (TAT), 25, 28, 31,
        37, 79
    defined, 162
    revving up and,
        130–131

toxins:
    children and,
        175–178
    defined, 22, 43
    fat as storage for, 14,
        22–27, 161–162,
        167–178
    environmental, see
        environment
    fungal, 54
    metabolism of,
        157–159
    PFR Syndrome and,
        23, 28, 162
    see also drugs; food
        additives; pesticides
tranquilizers, 172, 191
Tylenol (acetamino-
    phen), 159

UDMH (unsymmetrical
    dimethylhydrozine),
    66
Uniroyal, 66

vacuum cleaners,
    116–117
vegetables:
    pesticides and, 61, 63
    in PFR diet, 88, 96
vitamin(s):
    A, 157
    B, 59, 157
    C, 93, 94
    D, 157
    E, 59

vitamin(s) (cont.)
    liver's storage of,
        156–157

walking, 128–129, 133
Walnut Acres, 105
warming up, 78, 122,
    126–130
    in week-by-week
        action plans,
        142–144
washing, 113–114
water, 106
week-by-week action
    plans, 95–96,
    137–147
    detoxification,
        139–140
    maintenance,
        146–147
    mobilizing fat,
        145–146
    preparatory, 138–139
    recovery, 140–142
    revving up, 144–145
    warming up, 142–144
weight problems, see
    obesity
weight training, 153
Welch, Raquel, 151

yeast, 85
YES foods, 96–98, 100
yoga, 124–125

zinc, 92, 93, 157